Confessions of a Botox Babe

MARY YATES

Mary Yates is a woman who's not afraid of controversy. She was the most outspoken student nurse in her year, and is both admired and notorious for speaking her mind. In Confessions of a Botox Babe, Mary is searingly honest – and this time she's confessing about her life.

Based on a true story and told in her inimitable, unapologetic, and forthright style, Mary tells us her uplifting and inspirational life story, explaining how a working class girl from the West Midlands exceeded her parents' expectations to gain the professional respect she demanded, becoming a nurse and a practitioner armed with botox, for both herself and her clients.

Featuring Mary's sharp humour, Confessions of a Botox Babe is filled with shocking revelations about her life, and shows a vulnerable side of the woman behind the red lips and botox syringe. Whether regaling us with stories of her nursing, her non-surgical cosmetic business, her beloved children, her adventures in searching for lasting love, or her battles with money and mental health, this is a memoir that's guaranteed to result in laughter lines, which may have you reaching for the Botox yourself!

Copyright © 2017 Mary Yates
Cover Art by Garrett Leigh @ Black Jazz Designs
© 2017 blackjazzdesign.com

All Rights Are Reserved. No part of this book may be used or reproduced in any manner whatsoever without written permission, except in the case of brief quotations embodied in critical articles and reviews.

The author acknowledges the trademark owners of various products referenced in this work, which have been used without current permission. The publication/use of these trademarks is not authorised, associated with, or sponsored by the trademark owners, and does not represent any official endorsement of the products, only the personal and fictional narrative use and opinions of the author.

CONTENTS

1.	Introduction	1
2.	My visit to the General Medical Council	7
3.	My childhood – a baby in Birmingham	14
4.	Going to the wrong school	22
5.	Working with animals – though not how you think	30
6.	Finding a career – training as a nurse	36
7.	Developing my career in the NHS	47
8.	Working with homeless people	55
9.	Husband Number One	59
10.	Husband Number Two	66
11.	Having children – Joseph	75
12.	Having children – Kate	83
13.	Training to be a Botox Babe	90
14.	Being a Botox Babe now	98
15.	Mary's words of wisdom – Part One	104
16.	Depression	112
17.	Holidays and relaxation	117
18.	Internet dating – physicality and sex	125
19.	Husband Number Three	137
20.	Going bankrupt	140
21.	Divorcing Number Three	145
22.	Mary's words of wisdom – Part Two	151
23.	Why me?	161
24.	Mary's words of wisdom – Part Three	174
25.	What I've learned from bankruptcy and divorce	179
26.	Epilogue – now, and why I'm still a Botox Babe	187

CHAPTER ONE

Introduction

I've been obsessed with my appearance right from when I was a little girl. And why not? When I was five years of age, my mum and dad had an open fire, and I was still sucking a dummy at night. One night Mum tapped me on the shoulder. 'Mary, I think you should throw that dummy on the fire and I'll buy you a mascara.'

Straight away, I spat out the dummy and threw it on the fire. I knew what a mascara was even at that age and that was much more fun than the bloody dummy.

'Good girl,' Mum said and handed me the mascara. In the mirror, she showed me how to put it on, and soon afterwards I was laying it on thick.

So the Botox Babe was born at five years old and I haven't looked back since!

Even back then, as a little girl, I knew the importance of appearance and wanted to make myself look the best I could be. Even though by rights, at that age, I shouldn't have been sucking a dummy still, I didn't know any other kids my age who wanted to play with mascara. In fairness to my younger self, I didn't really play with the make-up, I took it very seriously. I knew how important looking good was.

I asked, 'Why should I wear mascara?'

'Look at my eyes,' she said.

As I was staring at them, she blinked.

'Long eyelashes make your eyes look bigger. It emphasises the wide eyes. It opens up the eyes.' She closed one eye and pointed to her green eye shadow. 'This matches my dress and makes my eyes look more blue.'

I sat in silence, transfixed by what she was saying, allowing every word to stick to me. I'd never heard anything I wanted to take so seriously before. All the things she'd said about emphasising shape and size of eyes were similar to what I would be telling my cosmetic procedures clients many years later, when I explained fillers and Botox procedures. So without even knowing it, Mum was training me to be a Botox Babe, right back then!

Why have I written this book?

Well, I always say if one person tells you something, it's up to you whether you take their advice or not, but if three people tell you the same thing, you'd better bleedin' well take notice. When I was at the height of my internet dating madness, in 2008 – I just used to get on a plane and go and meet people in Italy and Spain and random places like that – there was this one time I was in Italy and I got chatting to these two girls and one said, 'What's your name again?'

'It's Mary Yates.'

'Mary Yates, I want to read your book. When you write it, I want to read it.'

It was only when the fourth person who I'd never met before said they wanted to read my book, and told me that they had to hear my story, I thought I'd better bloody well do something about writing it. Which I have, and which is why you're reading it now!

The main reason for me writing this is because I want to make people laugh. With my life, I love laughing. I love hearing people laugh and I love making people laugh and it does work really well. I like to laugh a lot. I love to tell jokes and cheer people up, you know? I hope, with the story of the best bits of my life, you can learn something about living your life, about not worrying and sitting around thinking about doing things, about just grabbing life by the balls and living it. I've done some stupid dangerous things, but I can tell you, I've never been bored.

A life half lived, or not really lived, is a life wasted as far as I'm concerned. If you want to do something, just go ahead and do it. If it doesn't work, you can always change things and try something different.

When I was a nurse working in a hospital, I got talking to this chiropodist woman. I think they're called podiatrists now, but whatever, she was a woman who looked after people's feet. I said to her, 'Did you hear about the man that broke down on the motorway?'

'What happened?' she said.

'Well, he broke down on the motorway and this guy stopped and said, are you a mechanic? And he said no, I'm a podiatrist, and the man who'd broken down said oh, that's good, can I have a toe.'

And the podiatrist just looked at me, not laughing, not even smiling.

I said, 'You're supposed to fucking laugh now, that was funny! Tow as in pulling the car and toe as in on the foot.'

The thing is, once you've got to explain the joke, that's it dead and buried, isn't it? Also, not everyone has an actual sense of humour. You can't teach someone a sense of humour, you've either got one or you haven't.

I think if you can make people laugh, it makes them feel better. And me as a nurse, I spent a lot of time making people laugh, and it's quite addictive. I believe laughter is the best medicine, without a shadow of a doubt. I know it's a bit of a cliché and it's obviously not me who originally said that, but as someone who's been a nurse and looked after thousands of people, who's done cosmetic procedures on many people, and who's been through her fair share of challenges in life, I know how important it is to be able to have a bleedin' good laugh about something, 'cos otherwise, what's the alternative? Crying? Oh, just shut up!

That's not to say I've not done my fair share of crying too – more on that later – but after all, I'm still here, laughing, to tell the tale. Laughter helps me get through difficult times in my life. I just think having a good laugh is so important and I like to try and surround myself with people who have a sense of humour. I can't be doing with miserable bastards.

Of course, even I get down, but to lift myself up, I like to hear people laugh and I keep taking the bleedin' tablets! I've got through a lot of difficult things but I'm still here to tell the tale. You know, the kids' father, Husband Number Two, was horrible, controlling, violent, and although it was very difficult, and I was mainly laughing on my own then, laughter certainly helped me. If it wasn't for Husband Number Two, I wouldn't have the kids. And luckily my two kids are just brilliant, they're good looking kids, well educated and doing very well.

As I've written this book, I've relived all the funny, scary, mad, difficult, terrible things I've lived through so far in my life. It's made me realise there are two things I've aimed for during my life, since I was a child, right through to today: I've always wanted to lead a life that was more interesting than my parents' lives. Don't get me wrong, I loved my parents and they gave me a wonderful loving childhood, but it wasn't very exciting or challenging. They worked in the same factory job for their whole lives and never went abroad on holiday, just always staying near home.

The second thing that's driven me to fly all over the world, meet up with random strangers I've met on the internet, be married and divorced three times, is my search for a man who's as passionate as me. I've not yet found a man who can match me, so anyone who wants to apply for the job, answers on a post card to me!

These two strong desires have kept me striving, travelling, living, loving and exploring my life right up to now. I believe if I'd have been happy to live a life like my parents', I'd have worked in a metal factory like they did, and married someone who was all right, and would still be married, and probably bored shitless. But I didn't and that's why I'm telling you this story – the story of what made me into the Mary I am today. I hope you enjoy it.

I've also included in the story some of my words of wisdom. The thing is, having got through as much life as I've been through, I can't help being opinionated about certain subjects, and I want to share my thoughts and feelings with you on a wide range of subjects, from the problem with mobile phones to clairvoyants and marriage, love, and even revenge. You see, I can't keep my mouth shut if someone asks me about something, so I'm not going to keep my mouth shut in my own book, am I?

You can agree with me or disagree with me, I couldn't give a shit. You see, I'm one of those Marmite people, you either love me or you hate me, and if you hate me I don't give a flying fuck – and I've had a fair few of those too!

However, a few words about my age. I am sensitive about this and I've deliberately not included my year of birth in the book. You see, I like to lie to people about my age – it's the only thing I lie about,. It's only a little white lie really. Lady Mary is as old as her hair and a little bit older than her teeth, and that's as much detail as you're getting about my age. What's the point in having all this cosmetic surgery if I then tell everyone how old I really am? Besides, it's rude to ask a lady her age, and I am a lady. A lady who likes to say yes, but you'll hear more about that later.

This book covers my whole life, but because I didn't want it to be as long as War and Peace (which I've not read either, but the TV series was bloody well long enough) I've focused on the funny, the sad, the highlights, and the lowlights. So, a bit like my body, the story's been cut and grafted. I've also played about with the time line, so you don't start with me in my mother's womb and follow me right up to today, because who's bleedin' well got time for that? I've arranged the story to show how each of the major events in my life affected the next step I took: not getting into a private secondary school at eleven, working with animals and then training to be a nurse, searching for a passionate man, and then realising he wasn't so passionate and was a boring bastard, searching for another passionate man who ended up just being a bastard, my children and how that's affected how I feel about love, and how the children led me into becoming a real life Botox Babe – and eventually becoming bankrupt.

I've just re-read that paragraph, and it makes it seem like I planned it all. Like I had a big life plan and one thing has neatly led to the next. Let me reassure you, I didn't have any plan. I just dealt with things as they came to me. I've followed my heart in love, life and work, wherever it's led me. So don't think you've got to have some big life plan to lead an interesting life like I have!

Because laughter's so important to me, I hope it's gonna be a funny book, because some of these things that have happened to me are just bloody hysterical. The anecdotes, scenes from my life, and situations in this book are true, things that have really happened to me. However, the names, places and exact details have been changed and expanded or, in some instances, made up completely to protect the privacy of others who are still alive, to help illustrate a point, or just to make a better story. Including the pen name Mary Yates, a pseudonym to protect my own identity! I don't believe you should ever let the truth get in the way of telling a bloody good story and making other people laugh.

I want to dedicate this book to my darling, wonderful, demanding, complicated, beautiful children: to Joseph and Kate, love you both so much, this book is for you, lots of love from Mum.

And last but not least, thanks to you, the reader, for buying this book and letting me tell you about my life as a Botox Babe.

Mary Yates
xxx

CHAPTER TWO

My Visit to the General Medical Council

In 2016, wearing a bright red dress, white fur coat, high red stilettos and bright red lipstick, I went to the General Medical Council in Manchester – the GMC – the body all doctors and surgeons have to be a member of, to practice as a doctor or surgeon. You're probably wondering why was I, a nurse, going to the GMC? Well, I wanted to view this hearing about a doctor I used to work with. It's all open to the public, just like a court.

I hadn't seen Dr Mohammed for eight years and I paused outside the white six-storey building, checking the enormous clock above the arched double doorway. I had plenty of time. The first floor windows had white Roman columns separating the middle window from the ones either side.

I walked up to the ground floor reception past marble covered walls, with green marble columns on either side of a dark brown reception desk. A skylight filled the room with sun and I was impressed the receptionist could read her computer screen. She explained I had to go to the seventh floor for the GMC hearings.

The hearing room was filled with pale wooden benches and black chairs laid in a U shape, and at one end stood a separate bench with a chair behind it. In the chair sat the doctor.

I thought it was a shame that Dr Mohammed seemed to have let himself go a bit now. He was quite a fat bastard, not like how I remembered him years ago when we'd worked together.

When Dr Mohammed caught sight of me looking down on him from the public gallery, I was looking like the dog's bollocks. His bloody eyes nearly fell out of his head. I just sat there smirking. He'd been declared bankrupt for £876,000 and I knew he'd been fiddling the NHS out of loads of money.

This was the doctor who'd ripped me off for about £100,000 worth of cosmetic work and loans. We worked together for eight years doing NHS and cosmetic work.

I really hoped the GMC were going to strike him off so he wouldn't be able to practice medicine again, because although he was under all these supervision orders, he'd broken them.

I listened to the hearing, where they went through the evidence of what he'd been doing in this cosmetics business, alongside his NHS practice, but they didn't strike him off. There was me, thinking justice would prevail, but sadly the law prevailed, and there was 'insufficient evidence' to strike him off. So now he's back, still working in the NHS.

But for me to actually sit there as they went through the case, and told him their verdict – it was a wonderful feeling. It was proper closure on that chapter of my life.

Despite what he'd done to me all those years before, I was able to watch his case with my head held high, knowing that I was making my own money and looking fucking fabulous, all without him.

To understand the part of my life about Dr Mohammed, you have to start with my children, who are the most important thing in my life. It all came from me wanting to give them both private education. In 2003 I had been sending my son, Joseph, to private school since he was about seven or eight but, on my nurse's wages, I just couldn't afford to do the same for my daughter, Kate. It was so hard having two children and wanting to treat them fairly, but money wasn't growing on trees, and we had to eat and pay the mortgage – you know, other mad luxuries like that – so Kate had to go to a state school. But it didn't feel fair to me. I wanted both my children to have the opportunities private school would give them, which I hadn't been able to have at their age. It's what most parents want to do – give their kids more than they had as a child.

One afternoon, I was at a salon in Birmingham to have this electric treatment on my belly – they attach pads to my stomach and it pulses electricity making my muscles twitch, it's supposed to make you thinner, it's all shit really! – anyway, as I was lying there having this painful treatment, thinking why the fuck am I doing this, Eileen, who worked in the salon, told me about this woman in the shop next door who did Botox for her clients.

'What the hell's Botox?' I asked.

Eileen just shrugged and checked the pads on my stomach.

'Why the hell do the clients want it?'

Eileen shrugged again. 'All I know is, this woman walks out with 800 quid and then she spends it on handbags.'

Even though Eileen was no bleedin' use to me, I thought this had to be a sign, because eight hundred quid was so pertinent to me; it was the cost for one term at the private school I wanted Kate to attend.

It's funny how life throws things like that at you isn't it?

So as soon as I came home, I jumped on the internet and I found out what Botox actually was – it's an injection of a toxin into the skin which numbs the muscles. I wondered why anyone would want to have a toxin injected into their face, so I read on and found out the toxin numbs the muscles which cause wrinkles, leaving you with a wrinkle free face and forehead. I did a bit more looking about here and there on the internet, and eventually found this three day course for about £3,000 in Liverpool on Botox fillers and lots of other cosmetic injectables – by this point, I'd found out that's what they're called.

The course covered all sorts: Botox fillers, dental blocks, sclerotherapy, and facials. It's not like anyone could have gone on the course – you had to be a qualified healthcare professional, a doctor, a nurse, or something like that, so me being a qualified nurse worked perfectly. Sounds like a lot of money, but I tell you, I got the money back within a few weeks, In 2003, it was the early days of cosmetic procedures for ordinary people. I was one of the few people doing it that early, so I was really busy and I made shed loads of money and I never bloody well stopped working!

I was working full time as a nurse practitioner for Dr Mohammed and then I used to go off and do all these clinics all over the country. I used to drive all over the West Midlands, down to London and even down to bloody Plymouth as well, I was all over the shop. But I loved it. And most importantly, it meant I could afford for Kate to go to private school as well as Joseph.

So, what's that got to do with the doctor in the GMC and me in my fabulous red dress? I'm getting there! I was working for Dr Mohammed as his NHS nurse practitioner, when I did the cosmetic procedures training in Liverpool. I'd started working with him in his walk-in centre about three years before. Someone had told me a doctor was looking for a nurse and that the job came with a car. I thought, bloody hell, I could do with a new car, 'cos I was driving around in a £450 Ford KA at the time – bumpers falling off and bits of rust everywhere. So off I went and got the job with Dr Mohammed.

The doctor and I used to do this one cosmetic procedure together, called Isolagen, because he used to do the biopsies for it. One day, he asked me if I wanted to work with him in a separate business doing cosmetic procedures, so once I had the training, and had been doing my own cosmetic work, I thought why not? He ran a good centre, we worked together well there, and I thought it would be a good way to get more cosmetic work, and money from that.

Working with Dr Mohammed, he taught me how to borrow money. He also taught me how to go bloody bankrupt!

He'd say to me things like, 'Oh, I really need some money. Can you go to the bank? I need six and a half grand.'

And I was such an idiot, I used to just go and borrow it and give it to him, no questions asked.

Sometimes he'd say what he wanted it for. 'Some new equipment,' he'd say, or 'We need to buy the injectables in bulk, it's cheaper that way.' Or 'I need to go on training to do a new procedure.' He would often say, 'You go and talk to the bank for me, could you? You're so charming. They'll give you whatever you ask for.' There was always something he needed. Other times he'd just say he needed more money.

And off I would trot to the bank to borrow more bleedin' money. Honestly, it was madness.

Nothing ever happened between us sexually, but I'm sure Dr Mohammed was in love with me, because as well as bounding off each other at the clinic together – when I was always going off on the internet dating – when I would be off to Italy or off to Spain, he used to ring me all the time with, 'Oh you're still alive then?'

I'd think it was odd him calling me, when he didn't have anything about work to talk about. I would say, 'Well, obviously, you're speaking to me.'

And he would mumble on about something or another, and ask about what I was up to in Italy or Spain or wherever, and before he ran up my mobile bill too much I'd say, 'I'd better go, we can talk about it on Monday,' and put the phone down.

No, nothing sexual happened between us, we only had the business together – the cosmetic procedures clinic. There were three partners in the business, including myself, but it turned out he was such a crook.

It had all been fine at the walk-in centre, so I didn't think anything could go wrong. Well, you don't, do you? I'd been going great guns at the cosmetics work on my own. In one week, I banked £15,000! I could hardly believe it. It was paying for much more than my children's school tuition fees by then.

I was so busy, working at the clinic, doing my own cosmetics work, and working in the cosmetics business with the doctor, some weeks I didn't know who I was, where I was meant to be, or what I was doing. But somehow I managed to keep it all going and keep working and earning the money. I was just carrying on and carrying on and thought I was doing really well.

I didn't see any money from Dr Mohammed's cosmetics clinic – not a single penny for the whole time I worked with him. Although that sounds stupid of me now, at the time, I was so busy concentrating on actually doing the work, and Dr Mohammed was in charge of the business side, that I didn't think about the money really. I knew I was busy and that was all that's important in business.

And then, a very weird thing happened. In the middle of all this manic working and running about, one day I saw a clairvoyant and she said, 'You've gotta be careful, somebody's really going to stab you in the back.'

I didn't think anything of it. I couldn't imagine anyone who would stab me in the back. I see a lot of clairvoyants, and some of it comes true, some of it doesn't.

The next morning, back at the walk-in centre, I said to Dr

Mohammed, really blasé because I didn't believe it to be honest, 'Oh, apparently someone's going to stab me in the back.'

He stopped what he was doing and stared at me. 'It's not me.'

I didn't know why he was so serious, so I laughed, then said, 'Why would it be you?' Because as far as I knew then, we were running a busy, successful cosmetic procedures business together.

But nine months later, it fucking well was him, he stabbed me deep right between the shoulder blades!

One day, oh my God, I just suddenly woke up in a cold sweat and thought, shit! I owe all these people all this money, what am I going to do? I'd been so busy with the work, I hadn't had time to think about what I was doing. But each time I took out a loan from the bank, it was in my name. There wasn't one thing that made me realise something was wrong – it was a gradual build up of loan after loan, all in my name, and then it hit me. The debt was mine. I had to pay these people back and didn't have any way to do it, because I wasn't seeing any money from the business. Dr Mohammed looked after all that – the business side of things.

I took advice and was told to declare myself bankrupt for £165,000. It was shocking. It was like living in my own surreal dream.

It all came crashing down very, very quickly and such a lot of corrupt things about Dr Mohammed's business came out of the woodwork, later along the line. His accountant ended up in prison. Two of his business associates ended up in prison too. Dr Mohammed ripped me off. He never paid me the money I was owed for doing the cosmetic procedures. He ripped so many people off, and they still allowed him to practice. He slipped through the net every time. I mean, he is a real crook, that's why I was hoping he was going to be struck off by the GMC, because he is a bloody crook.

I had the Fraud Squad in my house, and I showed them the evidence of how much money Dr Mohammed was ripping off the NHS and do you know what? They did nothing about it. Nothing, nothing, nothing. I even went to a Conservative MP and told him the story. He wrote to the chief executive and they basically said it was me just being vindictive, or having a personal vendetta against the doctor. I'm not a petty person and the least of my worries was having some one-woman revenge on Dr Mohammed. I wanted to show how much he'd been ripping the NHS off over the years. I've got the letter somewhere. I have a file three inches thick. He went bankrupt for £876,000 and he owed me £100,000 for the work that I'd done.

Even all these years later, although I'd like to see Dr Mohammed struck off by the GMC, I realise I've just got to let it go.

My friend said that was the best thing to do, and maybe not knowing the verdict from the GMC would be best. I agreed and then said with a laugh, 'Even though I want to fucking kill the guy.'

Of course, I'd never kill anyone, never mind for something as stupid as money, but sometimes I get so upset thinking about what he did to me, how he took me for such a ride for so long, and for so much money – but that's some people for you.

Dr Mohammed got away with it, and they didn't charge him for anything. I don't even care any more there's no point in dwelling on that.

In the middle of it all, after I'd gone bankrupt and knew how much money he owed me, one night I saw him in traffic. I wasn't doing too well, financially, and was driving a little old Ford KA.

I slowed down and it looked like he was going to overtake me, and I'm so glad he didn't, because I was about to turn the car into him. I know I shouldn't have done, but that's the way I felt – at the time, in that moment.

It was really weird because as he was about to overtake me, he suddenly stopped, then turned off to the left. I don't think for a second he knew it was me. Of course, now I'm glad I didn't drive into him, because I'd have had to add a dangerous driving conviction to the things he'd left me with!

Life's taught me so much, and after all the impulsive, irresponsible things I've done, it's a wonder I'm still alive, so I'm not going to lose any sleep over Dr Mohammed and the GMC verdict. I'm going to move on with my life!

The best revenge is to live a good life and, my goodness, I've given that a good go over the years, as you're about to find out!

CHAPTER THREE

My childhood – a baby in Birmingham

I was born on the 20th October, at some point in the 20th Century, at home in Great Barr in Birmingham.

I'm a Libra. I'm a sort of Margaret Thatcher, she was a Libra too. She's definitely a Libra and so am I. Librans are sociable, persuasive, independent, forceful, self-motivated and natural leaders. We're also known for being artistic, refined and affectionate, as well as fashion-conscious and attractive. On the minus side, we can also be bossy, demanding, and carried away with outer beauty to the extent we ignore some people's inner beauty. As I said, I'm a real Libra!

Anyway, there was a midwife helping Mum get me out and into the world, and it was handy Dr Harris's surgery was on the opposite corner from our house, because he popped round afterwards to see how Mum was doing with baby Mary.

My parents were dead set on calling me Harriet, and my five year old brother, David, said, 'No, no, no, don't call her Harriet, call her Mary!' So it's his fault! Whether it was the old Mary and Peter Pan thing, I'm not sure. The children's story was out at the time, so maybe David wanted me to be his Mary.

My relationship with my brother was, and is now, good. We had a great time growing up together. Now we get on well, even though I don't see him very often. but we talk every week.

However, when we were growing up at home together we did sometimes fight. I remember my mum bought me this thing for Christmas – something called an Etch A Sketch, which you sort of doodle and draw with - on Christmas Day. I smacked David over the head with it and split it open, leaving my brother with a massive great bruise on his head. I got a right telling off. I think he was probably annoying me, you know, like older brothers do! I'm sure he deserved it at the time. Normally I got on with him when we were children – only the odd fight and argument, like all kids really.

Mum and Dad didn't treat us differently because we were a boy and girl, but they were strict with us. giving us a clip round the ear if we were badly behaved. Now, I often hear myself saying to my kids, 'I would've never spoken to my mum the way you speak to me.' If I had, I would get a clout round the ear. And I think times have really changed with parents and kids.

My parents were quite strict, but they were fair too – we got what we deserved. Mum was the strict one, the one that would clout me from time to time, not often. It didn't do me any harm; it's not like they were walloping us with the cane or slipper, it wasn't like bleedin' Oliver Twist.

Mind you, when I was about five, I slipped and split my eye open on the door handle of the cooker. It's one of my earliest memories. Mum picked me up and carried me over to Dr Harris in his surgery just over the road. He stitched me up there and then, no ambulance, no hospital, all sorted. I can remember it like it was yesterday – it bleedin' well hurt!

Overall, it was a nice childhood. But I never, ever had any of my friends to stay at my house and I never stayed at anybody's house. I don't know why, but it's just something that never happened. I suppose the friends I had were all local so we didn't have to stay in each other's houses. Now, with my kids, they're used to bunking over at other people's houses, but I never did. I don't regret it at all, I suppose it was because we led more local lives than nowadays.

When I was a child, we always used to go on holiday in England – caravans in Wales, going to the beach in Cornwall, once we even went to Butlins in Bognor Regis, that felt proper posh!

My dad used to go fishing with us as children. And, in fact, even now I love fishing, I went recently with a friend and I find it really relaxing, it's fabulous. My kids even love it as well, funnily enough, all from Dad. With Dad we used to go on these fishing trips quite often and then he used to tell me off: 'You're eating the fish cheese again! Stop it!'

I'd eat all the cheese that was meant for the fish. I used to sit by the side of the lake, next to Dad, and I'd eat this mouldy old cheese he'd cut up into little pieces to use as bait. God knows why, when there was plenty of fresh cheese back at home! I think I found fishing so relaxing that I didn't realise the cheese was mouldy or it was meant for the fish. I can't even look at a piece of mouldy cheese now without gagging!

When I was a teenager, we all used to wear miniskirts and big platform heels and my parents thought it looked so stupid.

'What you doing going out looking like that?' they'd ask.

'It's called fashion,' I would reply with a smile.

I liked to follow the fashions at the time – you do when you're a teenager, I think. I used to spend any spare money I'd earned on clothes. Looking back now, some of the clothes were very short, very tight and very brightly coloured. I can understand why my parents thought I looked stupid, but I managed to escape without any major fashion disasters.

My friend Sandra and I used to drink cider and sherry and go ice skating round the rink, pissed as farts, which was hilarious. I started dating at fifteen with this boy at school. He was nice, something to cheer me up at school when I was pretty unhappy. And then when I was sixteen, many moons ago, I went to Salou in Spain on my first holiday without my parents. I went with two friends who were two years older than me, but I had the best time, of course.

I met this Spaniard called Francisco – dark hair, dark eyes and the smell of dusky nights. After I'd gone home he wrote me a letter saying he wanted me to marry him, have ten children, a horse and a dog. I remember thinking at the time, when I read the letter, I didn't mind the kids, but I wasn't giving birth to a horse or a dog, so I didn't write back to him. Francisco was fun while I was on holiday – the classic holiday romance I suppose.

My grandparents on Mum's side were Katherine and Jo. So my son is Joseph and my daughter is Kate. Nan and Granddad were big and jolly – big boned as they say. They had loads of bloody kids, so they must've loved each other. We saw a lot of them when

I was growing up. They were happy people, and my nan used to sing to my granddad, which would drive him mad. She used to sing, 'Oh but we have no bananas, we have no bananas today!'

'Shut up, shut up, you silly cow!' he used to say.

Nan used to make bread pudding and toffee, she was always cooking and singing in the kitchen. She had twelve children – that was normal back then – but one died when it was born. The sad thing is, every one of their children is dead now, they didn't live to old age. But I've got a lot of cousins and we keep in touch, because it's such a big family.

My grandparents on dad's side were very different. His name was Joseph and she was Mary. I've never met that Joseph though, because he died before I was born. Joseph and Mary had two children, my dad and his brother. But I used to sometimes see Mary, my other nan, she was from Lancashire. I didn't see that much of her, because she lived much further away than my other grandparents. It's sad, but I don't remember a great deal about her. I don't have any vivid memories of her from my childhood. I hadn't seen her for a long time and I visited her as an adult and she looked like she'd just gone – like she'd died already, even though she was still actually alive. She was so old, it was very sad. I feel terrible because I can't even remember when she died. Isn't that weird?

Mum was one of eleven children, and she was seventy one when she died, she lived to the oldest age of all her brothers and sisters. Nowadays seventy one isn't really old, but back then it was.

When my dad came back from the war, they wouldn't let his brother in the house – I remember him telling me. He never told me why, though. Families can be funny things.

Family was important to Mum and Dad; they were married for fifty years and, growing up, we saw lots of our uncles aunties and cousins. We're still quite close now, the cousins, and I think it was spending time together as children that means we stay in touch now.

Mum was quite loving but we never hugged and kissed each other. We weren't what I'd call a huggy family, if that makes sense. I don't think families were so huggy back then as they are now, it was all this British stiff upper lip, or maybe it was the war where you didn't talk about emotions or feelings then.

I think I'm definitely more huggy and kissy with my children than my parents were with me.

My mum was the one who always used to whiz down the road every night to take Granddad his dinner; she was the caring one. When granddad came to live with us for a while after Nan died, Mum would look after him, and then when Granddad moved back home Mum used to take his meals to him every day.

Mum was like a nurse, she was a carer for everybody. She was another one like me, she always helped everybody out. Mum was very clever mathematically, she had a very fast brain and, hopefully, I've got a bit of that off her as well as the caring temperament!

The night before Mum died, we were at the hospital visiting her and this doctor walked up to us as we sat by her bedside and said, 'If she goes home, she's going to die.'

Mum said, 'Mary, come here.' She beckoned me forward with her hand. She said into my ear, her voice horse and quiet, 'Tell him arseholes.'

So I pulled myself up to my full five feet nothing of height and turned to the doctor. 'My mum said arseholes, now piss off.'

I put a complaint in about that doctor afterwards, he wasn't helpful, not what you want when your mum's at Death's door.

Mum wanted to be at home. In the end, funnily enough, the doctor was right because Mum went home and she did die the next day. But it was what she wanted – to pass away at home.

The day she died, my father phoned. 'You're mum's going.'

And I just dropped everything. I was in the walk-in clinic at the time, but I dashed round in my car and as I pulled up on the drive, my brother pulled up at exactly the same time, and the nurse came running out and said, 'She's gone.' Unbelievable, really, I'd missed it by seconds.

She died of cancer in 2000. Mum never took a tablet in her life, didn't complain or anything, she was really just a strong person, she wouldn't take the painkillers.

I'm like that too – about life generally. I don't believe in shying away from pain and problems, I just plough on through it. I've got that from Mum.

I've got my father's sense of humour because he was always cracking a joke, or doing a practical joke, or winding somebody up. As an old man, I used to take him to the hospital and he'd point at a black doctor and say, 'It's another nig-nog there.'

I would tap him on the shoulder and say, 'Shuttup, Dad, that nig-nog's gonna see you in a minute. He's going to try and make you better, so less of the bleedin' nig-nog.'

Although I know it's wrong to talk about people like that, that was his generation. He'd grown up through people saying the n word, then coloured and then black. How was he meant to keep up with it all? Nobody ever sort of challenged him. I mean, he fought for this country, if he wanted to say nig-nog that was up to him, I suppose. He didn't mean any harm in it, it was just the word he'd got used to saying as a kid.

Dad just liked to laugh. Not filthy, I mean my mouth's like a sewer but his wasn't. He didn't like swearing, not like me, I swear like a pissed sailor when I get going!

Every week I used to take my dad out of the house for a day because, after Mum died, it became harder and harder for him to go out alone. By this stage he was a bit wobbly on his feet and quite deaf, bless him, and he saw Husband Number 3, the Turkish man, and said, 'He's only about twenty five.'

'There's nothing wrong with your eyes then!' I laughed.

Everybody loved my dad, he liked to take part in the community where he lived. In Great Bar, because he'd lived there most of his life, he knew everybody, was always down the pub, at the shop, down the working men's club, chatting to people, having a laugh with them. He was kind and would help anybody if they asked him. He worked hard at the factory all his life, and when he wasn't working, he liked to laugh and people used to laugh with him. He was always telling a funny story, or teasing people about little things. That's probably where I get my humour from. He was brilliant, a brilliant man and a brilliant father. Dad died in 2009.

It's such a shame because, you know, both my parents are dead now, and you can't bring them back, that's your lot, the end. I suppose I'm an orphan now. It's only after Dad died that I realised that. It sort of came from nowhere one day. I was telling a colleague at work that my dad had recently died, and he asked about my mum. I explained she'd gone too. And then it hit me. I suppose I'm an adult orphan. You only get one set of parents, so it's important to spend as much time with them as you can and love them. Even though families are funny things and can drive you up the bleedin' wall, I'm glad I always got on with my parents and spent lots of time with them. For the younger readers out there, remember that. When your parents are gone, they're gone. Love them now.

Dad worked in the Imperial Metals Industry factory, and Mum worked in the same factory. My brother also worked in the same factory. They were all there, working together for many years. My mum got a gold watch when she retired, after forty odd years. Dad got a carriage clock after his forty five years. And then my brother was also there for years. My parents didn't drill into me that they wanted me to do better; they were working class people and just sort of went along with everything. They showed me that you don't complain and you just get on with things. (In case you haven't picked this up yet, I like do have a complain. I love to report people for doing wrong. If service isn't up to scratch I'm straight there complaining).

Don't get me wrong, they were good parents, they showed me the right way. But they all worked in a factory. It was just me who was different because I didn't want to work in the same bleedin' factory!

My parents were pretty religious, I was christened as a baby and I used to go to Sunday school every week. We would sit in this cold dusty classroom on little benches in rows, and the priest stood at the front of the room reading out parts of the bible. We used to draw things that were mentioned in the bible, and discuss what we thought the main lessons were from that week's reading.

And then, after we finished, we used to creep into the even colder, much bigger church and sit on a pew near the back, behind all the adults who'd gone to church that week. My parents were always there, near the front of the church. Sometimes they'd turn around and watch me shuffling along the pew with the other kids. Occasionally we would go on trips – to other churches, or other Sunday schools, traipsing around graveyards in the freezing cold and looking at the names and dates on the grave stones.

I actually enjoyed primary school. It was like nursery, lots of playing and talking to the other kids, and a bit of learning and writing stuff down. Our primary school uniform was a grey short pleated skirt and a white shirt. Miss Holmes was my favourite teacher because there was something about her, I warmed to her.

'Mary,' Miss Holmes said. 'Your vocal chords will be worn out by the time you're twenty one. I've never known a little girl talk so much!' I was only five years old then.

I was always asking questions, putting my hand up or talking to other pupils, and chatting in break time. I loved talking to the other pupils, it was the best bit of primary school. Even though I liked her, Miss Holmes was wrong; my vocal chords are still going strong, all those years later!

Miss Holmes taught me spelling and arithmetic. I can remember learning my times table, singing each one in time until it stuck, right from the two times table to twelve twelves is a hundred and forty four! Even now, when I want to work out something I say the times table in my head until I get to the right one, and I know the answer – either that, or I use the calculator on my phone.

Miss Holmes taught us about the vowels, and the other ones – I can't remember what they were called, but I remember a e i o u are vowels – and that's stuck all those years later, good old Miss Holmes.

CHAPTER FOUR

Going to the wrong school

Even at eleven, I knew I wanted more from my life than what my parents had done. I didn't just want to leave school with the basics and then go and work in a factory all my life.

I knew I wanted to meet people, to try out different jobs, to travel around the world, to live more of a life than my parents had. And I knew that going to a good school would give me the opportunities, the connections, the better education to live a more interesting life.

Because of the opportunities it would have given me, I really wanted to go to a grammar school. But I didn't get into that grammar school because I didn't pass the 11-plus entrance exam, so I ended up at a comprehensive school.

Even then, I thought it was so unfair that someone who needed more opportunities and a better education couldn't get it because they weren't clever enough. Surely grammar schools should take on pupils who are hard-working and willing to learn, so they can teach them and make them more clever? If all they do is take clever pupils and make them more clever, how much good is that really doing for people? So that was the grammar school idea out the window for me.

An alternative to the grammar school was a private school. However, my parents couldn't afford to send me to one of them. Even for a normal everyday private school, not somewhere like Eton, the fees were thousands of pounds a year, more than what my parents would have spent on a new car.

On their wages from the factory, they had enough to pay their mortgage, and feed and clothe my brother and me, have an annual holiday in Wales, and that was about it. Like I said, we weren't poor, we didn't go without, but our childhood had the basics, and that was about it. So no fees for private school, when I could go to a comprehensive for nothing except money for the uniform. I had no chance.

I tried to persuade them how hard I'd work at the private school, how much I'd learn, how I knew it would be better for me, but as an eleven year old child, I had no sway with my parents. 'You failed the 11-plus, you're going to the comp,' Dad said. 'It was good enough for me and your mother and your brother, it's good enough for you.'

So I had to go to this comprehensive which was bleedin' horrible.

Going to secondary school was a big change for me. They say, oh, your childhood days are the best days of your life. Well they bleedin' well weren't for me.

Maybe how I felt about the school was coloured by not wanting to be there, but usually, once I've committed to something, I roll up my sleeves and make the best of it.

I tried to do this when I started at secondary school, but it was just not the right way of learning for me. I never studied there properly so I never reached my full potential. It was when I left school and decided to go down the learning on the job route, that I did all my learning.

Because I'm not a very academic person – I'm more practical – the school didn't see my potential. Maybe now, if I was a child, they'd have a test and find out I was dyslexic, or number blind, or something similar. But back then, you didn't have dyslexia and things like that. They thought you were thick and stuck you at the back of the class with a dunce's cap on.

Because I struggled with the academic learning, they sort of ignored me. The classes were enormous, about thirty five pupils in each class, so when I didn't understand something the teacher didn't have time to explain it to me. She had to keep the rude pupils quiet and get through the lesson for the day. They stuck me in a corner and left me to it, so I wasn't engaged, wasn't interested in what they were teaching me.

And of course, because I didn't understand what they were

teaching I fell behind, which made me even less engaged, and so I fell further behind. It was a vicious circle. I remember in this one class, I was so far behind I didn't understand anything the teacher was talking about. I put my hand up to ask a question and the teacher ignored me. Eventually I walked up to her at the front of class and said I didn't understand.

'Which bit?'

'All of it, Miss.' I replied.

She shook her head and handed me a colouring book and pack of coloured pencils.

I'm one of those people where, if it doesn't stick, you have to explain it in a different way. The teacher didn't have time to be explaining things differently for me, or the other pupils at the back like me. Sometimes the teachers did explain it again, just like before, but so much of it didn't stick with me.

I used to hear the words from their mouths and they went in one ear and out the other. I didn't have anything in the words I could grab onto to help me understand – they were just a stream of sound, with no meaning to them. The words slipped off me and fell on the floor like the coloured pencils I was given to keep myself busy for some lessons.

As I'd expected, the comprehensive school didn't have time to actually teach me. In my imagination, the other schools would have had classes of ten to fifteen pupils, and kind teachers with endless amounts of time to explain things in different ways to make sure everyone understood. Since sending my children to private school, I realise I wasn't too far off in my imagination then. Give me a wound to dress, or a practical problem to solve – a party to plan, a house move to organise, a house to build and I'm brilliant – but the academia stuff? The books and writing, I have to work very hard on, and even then it doesn't always come out right.

Despite the school, I was very good at maths, and human biology was my best subject. I've always been interested in bodies. For some reason my brain was very good with the maths thing – I suppose it's because it's numbers and not words. I enjoyed those subjects, but others I really struggled with. When I went to school, many years ago, using the ITA – which I've just found out all these years later, stands for Initial Teaching Alphabet – you were taught to join up letters A and E, and then you had to learn to write properly.

It felt like learning to read and write two different ways and, unsurprisingly, I didn't understand it and found it really difficult. I remember just about getting the hang of the joined up A and E, and then being told they could be separate too, and how you could pronounce them differently depending on something else. To be honest, it's a wonder I can read and write at all nowadays for the rigmarole they put me through at school with the ITA and one thing and another!

The secondary school uniform was different from primary school: black blazer, grey skirt and white shirt. The uniform was the best part of secondary school; I'm a very uniformed sort of person, If I'm doing my job, I have to wear a uniform to be professional. Even now, I love wearing the uniform, especially with my name on it. I think it's really important that people know who you are and who they wanna complain about if they want to! The good thing about the school uniform was it made everyone the same, there was none of this designer clothes stuff like nowadays. I used to go to school with a Roy Cropper bag – the Coronation Street character. It was a rectangular bag with one strap that went over my shoulder, no logo, no colours, nothing. It might as well have been a carrier bag.

Because school was so useless for me, I did all my learning once I'd left. I suppose that's why, since I've had the choice as an adult, I've striven to give my two children the best opportunity I can with the private education.

In my view, just as I believed at eleven, I do still believe education is the best thing you can ever give your kids because it makes such a big difference to their lives. I always really wanted my children to have chances in life, chances I didn't have.

The school was horrible while I was actually there, as I've explained, but it was also awful for me after I left, because I knew I hadn't reached my goals or my potential there. I wanted to do so much more, but it never happened because I was too distracted, dumped in a corner and ignored.

When I was twelve, I was bullied for a little while at school. But then I stood up for myself. There were a couple of girls who tried to bully me – name calling and stealing my bag, stuff like that – but I overcame it. I ignored them and hoped they'd go away, and that was luckily what actually happened.

I don't want you to think I'm having a big long whine here. Secondary school wasn't all bad. I enjoyed drama – just like in real life, I suppose! I used to be in plays at the old repertory theatre in Birmingham and I was a member of the local acting society. I played Bubbles Laverne, an arty stripper. So I did do a bit of acting while I was at school, which was quite good fun. It was a practical creative outlet for me. It was such a godsend in comparison with the reading and writing about books and the capital cities and one thing and another. I really felt I could become myself when I was on stage. I didn't have to pretend I understood, or sit quietly in the corner – on stage I could run around and talk at the top of my voice, dressed up in costume, and have a great time. Acting was creative and interesting and, more importantly, fun.

I've not done any acting as an adult – but I just do that every day now, I think! When I left school at sixteen, one of the drama teachers wanted me to go to Switzerland to study acting, but I decided it wasn't for me. So I went off and worked with animals and nursing and stuff. I'm a bit of an actress now though – in my own way.

Even with some of the more practical things, I struggled at school. Some of them didn't feel like fun, even though they were practical and by rights, I should have been good at them. They felt like drudge, like hard work, like the sort of thing you'd ask someone else to do, unlike acting. I wasn't sure why I'd need to know how to cook or sew, because what I wanted to do with my life didn't need those skills.

I'd watched Mum cooking the dinner every night when she came back from work at the factory, and thought it was a shame she didn't have someone to do it for her. One night she was darning one of Dad's socks and she fell asleep in the chair even though it was only about seven o'clock. Her dress had patches and stitches from where she'd mended and fixed it over the years. I remember thinking that I wanted to earn enough money to buy myself a nice dress and to be able to have someone else cooking for me.

One day I said to Mum, 'We're doing cooking today at school.'

She must have known I would be a disaster, so she sent me in with a packet of pastry and a tin of apple. 'Make us an apple pie, love,' she said.

To be fair, it turned out quite well. You pour water in the pastry and shove the tinned apple into the pastry and, hey presto, an apple pie!

I remember doing something called a beef cobbler. It had cobbles on top, like dumplings, laid on top of the beef mince. It looked like baby food with little bits of carrot and peas in it, all covered in this white dumpling mix. I brought it home, a bit burned around the edges, and the minced beef tasted of flour. We chewed our way through one portion of it, me, Mum, Dad and my brother, and even though there was more left for another meal it mysteriously disappeared from the fridge. No, even then, I knew that cooking wasn't for me.

I was also pretty crap when it came to dress making and things like that. They tried to teach me dress making at school. I think I always knew I was more of a buying dresses woman than a making dresses one!

Sewing and cookery just didn't interest me at all. I thought they were for Mum's generation, not mine – I was the new generation, I was going to work and be equal to men, and not bother with all that faffing about in the home.

Once, at school, I tried to make a green trouser suit. It sounds hideous, let me tell you, it was hideous. I never finished it, which was probably just as well. It seemed to take so long to make clothes – cutting out the pattern, pinning the parts together, then sewing. I must have spent six weeks trying to make this trouser suit, hundreds of hours probably, and I remember thinking, if I worked, I could have earned the money to buy ten much nicer trouser suits by then.

I'm actually quite relieved nowadays that people don't tend to repair or make clothes. It's another thing I don't feel guilty about not teaching my children. Who needs to learn how to make a dress when you can buy a whole dress for less than twenty quid? You'd spend that buying the material and then you have endless hours of cutting and pinning and sewing, I really can't be doing with it.

When I was at home my mum always did all the cooking, washing, cleaning, as well as working in the factory. That didn't appeal to me at all. Now, I don't bother with cooking, I just eat out, buy a ready meal in, or get a takeaway. Who's got the time to be making a pie or a casserole?

Throughout my whole time at school, I didn't get any special awards. So I left school at sixteen with a few qualifications but not much else, and then I decided to go back to college and do English O level.

Although they were very, very good parents, I decided there was more to life than what they had. I got my first job, working with animals.

I'm so addicted to learning since I finished school, I'm actually starting a computerised accountancy course – don't ask me why, but I am! I signed up for it a while ago and although I thought I don't know what the bleedin' hell I'm doing this for, I think it keeps the old grey matter going and I might pick up some tips.

I'm more interested in the practical hands-on stuff. I know the value of learning, wherever you do it, which is why I've done my best to give my children the best education I could afford.

At the time, school was five years of hell on earth – kids are so dramatic! – and except for the drama lessons and maths, I left school with not very much. However, the feeling of wanting to live a life more interesting than my parents' has stuck with me to this day.

Although I didn't get the opportunities another school would have given me, I believe the experience of struggling through school has taught me to strive and get through other challenges life has thrown at me.

It's taught me there are more ways to get what you want, so although I didn't learn much at school, I learned there are hundreds of other things to know, and ways to learn that school doesn't teach you, and since school I've never stopped learning and teaching myself. Because this has taken me in so many different directions, it has meant I've lived an interesting life, far exceeding my parents' expectations. So maybe if I had gone to another school I would have had a much more predictable and less interesting life afterwards!

CHAPTER FIVE

Working with animals
– though not how you think

I'm very good at getting jobs. Whatever I apply for, I always get. And then I think, what have I done that for? I enjoy applying for jobs, trying to get them. At one stage I was writing out application forms every couple of weeks. I'd go to the interview, get the job, and think, OK, Mary, what have I done that for? It was a bit of an addiction, I think – I'd convince myself I've gotta get this job. I've no idea why, but I'm sure some psychiatrist could work it out for me!

I've always felt my job was important to who I am as a person. When I first trained to be a nurse, I couldn't wait to get the uniform, to have the badge with my name and job title on it. I also know I'm a bit of a self-confessed workaholic. I've always worked at least one job, since I was sixteen.

Sometimes I've worked a full time job, like when I worked as a NHS nurse, and worked weekends too on the market stall, selling handbags and luggage with my second husband. After the divorce, I still couldn't get enough of work – I worked in a GP practice, did my own cosmetic surgery clients, and worked on cosmetic clients with the doctor – so at that point I was actually doing three jobs!

Do I ever stop? Not really. Even when I had my children I was back to work as quick as I could. After my breakdowns or other periods of illness, I've still carried on working. I think, for me, work is like its own form of therapy. It gives me purpose, meaning, reason to my life. The main reason I work now, is for my kids – when they were younger I wanted them both to go through private school, so I worked for that. Now I want to make sure they have all the opportunities they could have to live a more full and better life.

Of course, I work for myself too – I like to enjoy the money I earn. I enjoy holidays, nice clothes, jewellery, a bit of pampering, eating in nice restaurants – the finer things in life, of course. And all those cost money, so that's another reason why I work.

I started full time work at sixteen, in an animal lab. Even though I was quite good at drama at school and one of the drama teachers, Mr Knowles, wanted me to study acting in Switzerland, I decided to go on holiday first with my friends – my first holiday with my friends. I was sixteen and I went to Spain with two of my sort of neighbours, girls who were a bit older than me. I went on that holiday and I came back and started work straight away. And yeah, it was a bit of a strange thing to go into, but I just did. Then when I was there I met Brian, who was my first husband.

I couldn't wait to leave school because I'd not learned much and didn't enjoy it at all – except maybe the maths and drama. As soon as I could leave, at sixteen, I knew I wanted to start work. I was done with learning how they'd tried to teach me, and I wanted to earn my own money and make my own way on my own in the world.

My parents had shown me the importance of working – they both paid for everything with their own hard work. My brother was working in the same factory as our parents, but I knew I wanted something different, something more interesting. I'm not a snob, don't get me wrong, there's nothing wrong with doing that sort of job. But I wanted to work with people. I wanted to work where I felt I could make a difference.

I wanted to prove to myself and everyone else that, even though I hadn't done well at school, I could do more than what was expected of me. It wasn't as if my parents actually said they expected me to work with them, but I felt like I was expected to follow suit, as my brother had done a few years earlier. I wanted to start myself on a path, living a life, that was more interesting than my parents'. And I knew that if I got a job up the road in the factory, I wouldn't manage that.

When my parents used to come home tired from work, and I'd ask them how their day had been, what had they done, hoping to hear about their colleagues, or people they'd helped , all I'd get was some stuff about the belt – the conveyor belt, I later learned – going too fast for them to keep up with, or being moved from one job to another a bit further along the line. Mum used to have nightmares about not being able to keep up with the conveyor belt and lagging behind. She'd turn and turn in the sheets, scrabbling with her legs, trying to keep up with the imaginary belt.

I remember thinking I didn't want my days at work to be filled with machines. I wanted to talk to people, to show how I'd helped someone or something at the end of my working week. I felt sorry for Mum getting herself in such a state about the conveyor belt. I knew I'd never care as much as that about a job in a factory and that would leave me feeling unfulfilled and bored. Mum and Dad never seemed bored with their jobs, they just accepted that as the way for them to pay the mortgage and put food on the table. I think it's because I was from a different generation – who grew up with women's lib and different expectations of what work could be. I didn't want a job, I wanted a career. Only, at sixteen, I didn't know what the career would be. So I applied and got a local job that was as different from the factory as I could manage.

I was an animal technician in a laboratory. Yes, it was one of those labs – where they do vivisection and experiments on the animals. Perhaps that's where I got my animal magnetism. Anyway, I saw the job advertised in the local paper and I thought, I'll do that – it's not a factory, that'll do me nicely.

I didn't do the vivisection but I looked after animals that were used for experiments. It was mainly rats, mice, rabbits, little animals like that, which somehow didn't seem as bad. I don't think I really thought about what they were doing to the animals then. I was young, and it was a job.

When at first I didn't have anything to do with the experiments, I managed not to think about them. As far as I was concerned, I was just looking after a group of animals, a bit like working in a big pet shop or little zoo. I was the zoo keeper for my own zoo! I think that's how I coped with it. I think I ignored the fact that the animals would disappear all the time and be replaced with a new set of animals to look after. It's amazing what you can put to the back of your mind when you're young. I don't think I'd be able to do it now, because I'd be too worried about all the animals. But as a teenager, I just got on with my work and didn't pay attention to the rest.

As well as the little animals, there were dogs they used for experiments. I used to steal the dogs, that is, I used to save them. I didn't want them put to sleep after the lab had finished with them – I wanted them to all live happily ever after. With the little animals, I could pretend they'd just disappeared, but the dogs were family pets, and when I thought about what they were actually doing to them, I was so sad I had to do something about it.

I was like some sort of vigilante, breaking the dogs out for their freedom. Everyone I knew took one of these rescued dogs. Mum and Dad had one, I had one, our neighbours had one. I even tried to palm one off on the milkman and the postman. I'd just get rid of one, give it away, and next time I was at work I'd be rescuing another one. I was a one-woman action Mission Impossible film, or maybe Charlie's Angels. That's a bit more glamorous, a bit more me. I was the Farah Fawcett of Birmingham, rescuing animals week after week, saving them from imminent death.

I would check until the coast was clear – there was no security guard – and then I'd cover the dog in my coat and smuggle it out under my arm if it was small. For the bigger dogs I used to wait until it was dark at night, sneak back into the lab alone, and just walk out with them, with a piece of string for a lead.

Technically I was stealing from the laboratory – they were very expensive, these dogs – thousands of pounds each one was worth, I was told by the receptionist one morning, when another had mysteriously gone missing. Unfortunately, the beagles were really stupid. I'd try to call them to leave with me and they'd just sit there in their little cages staring at me. My heart would be beating as I tried to be as quiet as possible and not attract the attention of my colleagues. Somehow I got away with it, time and time again.

I don't remember ever being told off or found out. Maybe the other staff knew and they ignored it because they thought I was doing a good thing, something they'd wanted to do but didn't have the guts, maybe? I've always been the sort of person who has to speak up if I see an injustice. Even though they were my employer and I was stealing from them, in my heart of hearts I felt saving the dogs was the right thing to do, so I kept on doing it.

I know in some animal labs they tested cigarettes by making animals smoke. Although we never did that, ours were used for all different surgical techniques and procedures. They used to try them out on them – to see if it could be used on humans. They'd try different types of stitches, or test out what would make the dog accept a donor kidney from another dog. It was really interesting.

After being there for a while, looking after the animals, I started asking lots of questions about what they did, why they were doing it, and if I could give them a hand, because I've always been gobby and asked questions. They used to let me stitch up the animals after the operations. I would even help out with the operations too, sometimes. So soon enough I wasn't just cleaning out animal cages.

I really enjoyed it when I helped out with the operations. I remember thinking, I could do this, or something similar, but with people, maybe, and I think that was the start of me thinking about training to be a nurse.

I used to watch one surgeon do kidney transplants on rats. These were tiny rats' kidneys, and he did the operation under the electron microscope. The man explained he was trying out this drug, which is quite well used now, to stop the rats from rejecting the kidney. They use it now in human transplants – hearts, eyes, kidneys, the lot.

I hadn't seen him for twenty five years, and I rang him one day about a patient that I had. As soon as I spoke to him, I went, 'Hello Malcom, you probably don't remember me.'

Without a pause or asking me who I was, he said, 'Mary, how are you?'

Because I've obviously got a very distinctive voice, and a distinctive personality too.

'How are you, Mary?'

'I'm absolutely fine darling. I've got this patient I need some help with.' And we talked about the patient and what I could do with her, and one thing and another. It was like I'd just seen him the week before for a drink.

Although the work in the lab was a bit disturbing when I thought about it, the people there were all lovely, very friendly, helpful, kind to me, just out of school, still a bit wet behind the ears, you know.

And among the colleagues, I met my first husband, another lab technician. I'd dated a few men beforehand, but when I met Brian I thought he was kind and caring, and that I'd met a man who was as passionate as me. I'd found my Mills and Boon romance novel ending, like I'd read about so many times as a teenager. Unfortunately, it wasn't that simple, but that's for another chapter.

I know some of you must still be thinking, how could I work in a laboratory where they were experimenting on live animals? In fairness, even though when I actually thought about what they were doing to the animals it upset me, I understood they were doing it for a bigger benefit – like the transplant drug or testing how well drugs worked. I knew they weren't doing the experiments for the fun of it. And although sometimes it upset me enough to steal the dogs, I enjoyed it, I cared about the work, I was interested in what I was doing.

I knew if I'd been working in the factory with my family I wouldn't have been interested in the work. Just hearing about my parents' days at the factory was enough to bore me rigid, never mind doing it for eight hours a day, five days a week. There was no way I'd have ever been able to follow them. Getting an interesting job that stretched me was my two fingers up at the school that had, as far as I was concerned, failed so miserably at giving me an education.

Working in the laboratory was definitely linked to why I eventually became a nurse. I remember thinking one day that I was interested in bodies, in biology and the health of the animals, so it made sense to see what I could do for humans. I'll be a nurse, I thought. After five years of being an animal technician I decided to be a nurse. Just like that.

Becoming a nurse was another step away from the factory, another step away from having just a job and towards having a career, a profession, which was more than anyone else in my family had ever achieved before. Nursing was another way I could make sure my life was bigger, broader, more interesting than my parents' had been. And that was the start of the next challenge I gave myself.

CHAPTER SIX

Finding a career – training to be a nurse

I'd been thinking I could do with a change from the animal technician work for a while, and then one day I told Mum, 'I want to be a nurse.'

'Really? Where's this come from?' she asked. She thought I was a bit crazy and frowned.

'I just want to be a nurse.'

'What do you wanna do that for?' she asked.

''Cos I really want to.'

She didn't know what to say to that, so she just stood there in the kitchen, arms folded across her chest, dinner half ready. I'd sort of come home from work and suddenly flung this at her. No wonder she didn't know what to say. As far as she was concerned it was coming from nowhere.

'I want to make the most of my operation skills on the little animals. I'm bored of animals I want to look after people!' And I just flew at it. I loved it, and even to this day I'm very passionate about it; always learning about something, always doing one thing and another new. Because that's the way I am. I've got a lot of energy for an old one. And I just like to keep going – very strange really.

I decided it was like a calling for me to be a nurse. All the people I worked with at the lab said, 'You should be an auxiliary nurse, you should be a vet.'

'No, no, no, I am not being an auxiliary nurse, I want to go and train, I want to be a qualified nurse!' Nowadays they call auxiliary nurses health care assistants and to be fair, they do the majority of the care – the washing and dressing, and taking to the toilet and feeding. It wasn't like that when I trained – a nurse did all those things too. I wanted to be a fully qualified nurse and nothing less.

When I started my nurse training, I left home. I bought my first property when I was nineteen with Brian, so I was actually living the other side of Birmingham from Mum and Dad. But we used to go and see them every week. They were fine, I think they were quite proud of me, they used to ask how it was going each week. I had a little Triumph Spitfire to get around in. I felt like I could do anything with my life – that's what it's like when you're young isn't it?

'You know, it's wonderful!' I would say.

'What they got you doing?' Mum and Dad would ask.

And I'd explain what I'd learned that week – doing bed baths, hospital corners on beds, learning about drug doses, everything. There was so much to learn and it was all so different, and I lapped it up, every bit of it.

Sometimes they'd go quiet when I told them about something quite technical, like blood pressure I'd learned about, or the temperature of the body, or about hydration, or how to do CPR if a patient had a cardiac arrest – which everyone else calls a heart attack.

Nursing was a million miles away from their jobs in the factory so sometimes it must have gone a bit over their heads, but I did my best to keep them up with what I was learning. I wanted them to see how much I loved it, the hard work, the studying, the shifts, the people, everything.

Nursing was probably something that my mum would have liked to have done but she just didn't do it. I think my mum, even though she always worked in a factory, was definitely a carer. She looked after my granddad, and one thing and another, perhaps she missed her vocation in life, I don't know. They were proud of me and I wish that my mum could have seen what I have achieved now.

I took two years to complete my nurse training in Bromsgrove General Hospital.

I finally qualified as a State Enrolled Nurse (SEN) and it was brilliant. It was in the days when you wore starched hats, which I used to love. To actually put a starched hat on as a trained nurse was such a proud moment for me, something I'd been looking forward to during the whole two years of training.

By then I'd got the bug for learning, for nursing, and I thought, I want to go on further to be a ward sister, to maybe be a matron, but I hadn't got the qualifications to do that. As a State Enrolled Nurse there was only so far up I could go, because I'd done the supposedly less academic nurse training route. I worked as a SEN for a while and used to watch the Registered General Nurses (RGNs) taking charge of the ward, being in charge of student nurses, that sort of thing and I thought – I could do that, and I'd be bloody good at it. I didn't have the initial qualifications to do the registered nurse course, straight away, so I did it the long way round – eventually.

It sounds a bit corny, but as well as the medicine and dressing the wounds with bandages and one thing and another, nursing is also the little things like being able to help somebody. And to touch somebody and hug them and know it's made them feel better. It's just wonderful, it's brilliant, absolutely brilliant. I loved it then. I love it, I do it now and I love it.

Some people say they could never do nursing because it's dirty or you're touching somebody else's body, or cleaning up somebody else's shit but, honestly, I don't find anything about nursing difficult. I get such a buzz from somebody saying thank you, or knowing I've made them feel so much better. When I first qualified as an SEN I went on nights. After those, when I came home, it was the best night's sleep I ever had in my life. I used to do three nights one week, four nights the next. I used to come home and get in bed and I'd be fast asleep within minutes, it was brilliant.

I'd never seen a cardiac arrest while I was training and then I was on this gynae ward (women's things) and this one night we had four cardiac arrests and four deaths! I couldn't believe it. Talk about throwing me in at the deep end. And there was this Chinese nurse called Nellie Ball who said, 'There's another one gone!'

'What?' I couldn't believe it because we'd already had three cardiac arrests at that point.

'Another one gone, come quick!' So we all ran down the ward with the crash trolley. We pulled the curtains round the bed and we put the pads on his chest and did chest compressions, and stood back for the electric shock to start his heart again. And oh, fucking hell, somebody else had died. I dunno what had happened, it was one of those nights. I remember coming back to the nurses station and writing up all the notes about what had happened, who'd done what, when they'd arrested, when the doctor had pronounced them dead. It felt surreal, writing it down afterwards because it was such an extraordinary experience. Just sort of one after the other, dying. It made me realise life can be short, and life's for living, and you never know when your number's up.

So after being a State Enrolled Nurse for a while, in the early eighties, I went to Oswestry in Wales, and did an orthopaedic nursing qualification. While I worked there I used to make homemade wine. I was still married to Brian at the time, and I used to take these demijohns of homemade wine into work. And this one night this porter got so pissed on my homemade strawberry wine, he tripped over, cracked his head on the side of the kerb, and he couldn't work for a week! There was blood everywhere, good job he's right outside the hospital I thought, and rushed him into A&E to be treated.

Oswestry has a really funny hospital because the main corridor was a quarter of a mile long. And they only had one crash trolley for when people had a cardiac arrest, which was right at the other end of the corridor. So if somebody had a heart attack at the one end of the hospital that was it, they were fucked, no chance, because by the time you'd wheeled the one crash trolley a quarter of a mile, they'd been gone for too long to do anything.

I remember I was on this one ward and I was walking down it with these stainless steel bowls and they were all shaking. I thought, fucking hell, I must have had a load to drink last night. I was actually quite worried. Thankfully, it wasn't me, it was an earth tremor. Apparently they get them in Wales too, as well as America and the other side of the world. Who knew?

I had so much fun at that hospital. There was a guy called Chong, and he was from Hong Kong and you used to have to do these rounds with the tetraplegic and the paraplegic patients where you had to turn them from side to side so they didn't get pressure sores on their bums from laying in the same position too long. This is a bit gross, but because these patients couldn't open their bowels to go to the toilet on their own because they had no feeling below the waist, you used to put suppositories up their bums and then you'd do a manual evacuation. It might sound like making everyone leave a building during a fire alarm, but trust me, a manual evacuation is nowhere near as glamorous – it involves removing faeces from a patient's bottom with your hands. Not my favourite job, but it was the only way these patients could go to the toilet. Anyway, this Chong was so fucking slow, I said, 'Chong, if you don't hurry up I'm going to stick these two suppositories up your arse.'

And he turned around and went, 'Mary, you talk a lotta shit!'

'That's where you're going wrong,' I replied. 'You don't want to be talking shit, you want to be manually evacuating it. Now get on with it, I'm getting old stood here.'

One morning I arrived on the ward and I thought, I must look good today. I checked my reflection in the mirror – normal, nurses hat, no make-up, white dress and sensible shoes. As I walked down the ward, all the guys had got erections, big lumps in the bed sheets, every one of them.

I asked Matron quietly, what that was about.

'It's not you, Mary, it's an autonomic thing. When they are paraplegic or tetraplegic you've only got to wash near the area and they often get an erection.'

'So it's not me?' I asked, with a wink.

'No, it's not you,' Matron replied. 'Now come into the office, and have handover with everyone else.'

Matron explained that they can't feel it, which is part of being tetraplegic or paraplegic. It's quite sad for them.

Sometimes we used to take these patients out to the pub for a change of scene, when the ward wasn't too busy. Some of them might have been in hospital for months while the hospital decided if they could go home and have people look after them. There were all sorts of reasons why they were on that ward – car crashes, motorbike accidents, falling off buildings, stuff like that. They'd have a drink at the pub and the nurses would wheel them outside in their wheelchair to empty the urine bag down the drain and then take them back in again for another drink.

Even though I said I love everything about nursing, there was one job I found difficult. While working at the orthopaedic hospital I was a plaster nurse and I was absolutely shit at it. No two ways about it, no point making bones about it.

I used to put these plasters on. and then saw them off again because I had put them on wrong. I think that was one of the worst jobs I ever had. I just couldn't fucking do it, no matter how hard I tried. I put them on the right bit of the body but I was crap at it – they didn't fit right, they were too short, too long, not tight enough. I absolutely hated it because, no matter how hard I tried, I was still as shit as ever.

I'm not sure why I was so bad at it, but I've never been one for putting up shelves, or pictures on the wall – it felt to me a bit too much like DIY. It was all about the plaster, and not so much about the actual patient, do you know what I mean? It felt to me like the arms and legs and hands being plastered might as well not be attached to a patient, because all we did in that department was plaster, plaster, plaster, no other sort of nursing. It was very repetitive – and I was repetitively shit. I didn't do it for very long, thank God. I left of my own accord. I realised my future didn't lie in being a plaster nurse, thankfully!

After the orthopaedic training, I came back to Birmingham and then I did my registered nurse training for three years. At that point I'd spent about five years training to be a nurse in various ways. After I qualified as a RGN, it felt so great to know I could be in charge of the ward, I could mentor the student nurses, I too could be a matron if I wanted.

During this part of training, I had to be assessed doing something called a total patient care which basically means washing, dressing, toileting, everything really for a patient who can't do any of their own care themselves. Mr Daniels, the nursing officer, was assessing me that day. Mr Daniels was married and he was very camp. He used to spend all his time striding up and down the ward, pulling the dead heads off the flowers as a sort of obsession or hobby.

'Come on then nurse, let's do your total patient care.' Mr Daniels collected his notebook and pen and followed me.

I walked to my patient, an eighty-odd year old gentleman, Mr Ice, on a geriatric ward. 'Come on then Mr Ice, we're going to give you a bath.'

'No, don't want one, don't want one.'

'No you'll be fine, you'll be fine. Get you nice and clean.'

We wheeled Mr Ice into the bathroom and lifted him from his wheelchair onto a shower chair which is a toilet seat hoist, so you can lift the patient up and down and wheel them around while sitting on the seat. I wheeled Mr Ice on the shower chair over the toilet so he could go before having a bath. 'Look, it won't be a minute, and then you'll be in the water,' I said to Mr Ice. I explained to Mr Daniels that Mr Ice always said he doesn't want to go but he always does.

'Oh yes, OK, you know the patient better than me, nurse,' Mr Daniels said

'Ok Mr Ice.' I lifted the shower chair seat up and wiped his bottom, then pushed him towards the bath. I'd been taught to always offer patients the toilet before having a bath, otherwise they could sometimes shit in the bath. I was feeling pretty pleased with myself at this point.

Mr Daniels stood by the side, making notes on his pad, scribbling away with his pen.

I got my breath back, because Mr Ice was pretty heavy being wheeled about on the shower chair. I turned the taps on, checked the water temperature with my elbow, just like I'd been told. I was just about to move Mr Ice over the bath and lower him into it when he did the biggest shit ever on the floor. It was about six inches tall and six inches wide.

I looked at it then I looked at Mr Daniels. 'Oh dear, I don't think he'd finished.' I cleaned it up. 'Oh dear, what a shame.' Then I lowered Mr Ice into the bath and washed him, even though he kept telling me to 'Bugger off, bugger off!'

'No, no, I need to scrub your toenails,' I said.

Mr Ice kept putting his legs up in the air.

I dried and dressed Mr Ice, put him back in a wheelchair and back to bed. All the while, Mr Daniels stood by the side, writing on his pad. I was relieved when he told me I'd passed the total patient care, despite the shouting and the shitting on the floor.

There was this guy, and he'd come into hospital and he and this girl, they'd won a load of money on the pools and he'd sort of blown all the money. When he was admitted into hospital, we put him in the bath to clean him up and he had so much flaky skin on his body – this is going to sound gross but it really happened – it blocked the plug hole up when we let the water out. I had to fish all the flakes of his skin out with my hands to let the water go down.

We put him on this water bed to prevent him getting pressure sores if he lay in the same position too long. When we made the bed, it was like sailing on the seven seas. One little knock at the foot end and there'd be a wave rippling up the whole bed, right up to his head. Anyway, the poor sod died, just as his visitors were coming in to see him. We pulled the curtains round to wash him and lay him out in a shroud for the family to see him.

I remember trying to wash this man on a water bed and it was absolutely hilarious 'cos he was slipping and sliding all over the place. There was me and another nurse and we were just laughing, because as we were trying to wash him, he was moving about all over the place. I pulled the man towards me while the other girl washed his back, but the water bed made him slip out from my grip, so he was on his back again. Then when we turned him the other way so I could wash him, the girl lost her grip and he slipped across the bed. Thank God the curtains were closed while we were doing this, while we were tittering. We got him washed eventually, even though he was rolling all over the bed.

It might sound a bit disrespectful but honestly, in nursing, if you can't have a laugh, you'd die. We cleaned him and laid him out for his family to view him dressed in the shroud. And it's true what they say – there aren't any pockets in shrouds so you might as well enjoy your money when you're alive!

After my RGN training, because I'm not one to let the grass grow under my feet, I did my district nurse training for a year.

District nursing is very different from nursing on a ward – you're travelling about from patient to patient across the geographical area you cover, doing a whole load of different things for each patient. One visit, I'd be injecting a patient who had diabetes with some insulin, and taking his blood sugar reading. Next, I could be bathing a bed-bound elderly patient and then I might be changing a dressing on another patient's legs from pressure sores. I loved it because it felt like I was my own boss – travelling around in my little car, visiting patients, and seeing them on my own, making clinical decisions in their best interests. District nursing has changed so much now. It's all targets and paperwork and not so much about patient care. But I won't go on anymore because that's another of my hobby horses.

To this day, I am still doing things training-wise because I just can't not. You can't stop, you have to keep learning, always keep learning. I'm doing a computerised accountancy course next week, I don't know why I'm booked onto it but I have! I've paid for it, so I'm definitely going. I must be mad!

When I was a district nurse – this was back in the days when nurses used to wash people in their homes – total patient care, I suppose I'd call it. Nowadays the washing is done by care assistants, but then it was part of a district nurse's job. Anyway, I went to a house to give this man a bed bath who was terminally ill. I walked into the bedroom and could see straight away he was dead – grey white in the face and not breathing and he'd got a hot cup of tea next to him. So I called the son-in-law into the room and I said, 'He's dead.'

'Is he?' He shook his head. 'Can't be.'

'Who's just given him a cuppa tea?'

'That's what I mean, he's got a hot cuppa tea, he can't be dead.' The son-in-law was struggling to grasp it, I think.

'No, that's what I mean, who's given him the tea, when he was already dead?' I looked at this man, not knowing how else I could put it to him.

And the son-in-law, he couldn't answer, he stood there with his mouth open, staring at me.

I broke the news to the man's wife and the daughter then I rang up the surgery and told the GP the old man had died.

Bless him, this GP said, 'I'll come straight away.'

About twenty minutes later, he rang the doorbell.

I opened the door – I was pretty relieved to have someone else to talk to because the family were all just sitting there in silence, staring at their tea. I closed the door behind me quietly. 'They've only gone and given him a fucking cup of tea.'

'When?' The GP asked.

'After he'd bloody well died.'

His jaw dropped.

'He's white and looks dead. I could tell he was dead as soon as I walked in, never mind putting a cup of tea next to him!'

I worked as a district nurse for over ten years and I used to do lots of rewarding things; things I didn't have to do, but because I'm me, I had to do, if you know what I mean.

There was an old lady I called on to check her leg ulcers, every week I used to visit her. After I'd finished one time she said, 'My cat needs worming – can you help me please?'

She didn't have anyone else who could help her hold it, or take it to the vet, so there was I, putting these worming tablets down its throat while she told it not to panic and that it would be over soon. It's a lovely thing to feel that you can help somebody, it's so rewarding.

During district nursing I got used to going into people's homes, seeing how they lived, helping them into the bath, making them some food, all sorts of stuff. Anyway, I remember this poor man had been discharged from hospital and he opened the letter and it said he'd got terminal cancer and he would go down really quickly. I couldn't believe they'd written that in a letter, no phone call, no appointment face to face, just a letter.

He was pretty stressed about it, what would he do, how could he make sure things were ready for when he died, and one thing and another. I told him to calm down and put this relaxation tape on and I made sure the fire was nice and warm. Before long the man and his wife were asleep.

To be honest, I was well relaxed too, just spending time with him, making sure him and his wife were OK – because when you get a letter like that, there's not much more you can do except chill out and make sure everyone's comfortable. In the middle of this sort of medication session I'd set up for them with the music, somebody came to the door. I saw who it was – double glazing salesman, got rid of him so the couple could carry on being well chilled out with the tape.

Anyway, the day he actually died, the family called me round so I could be there because they wanted me there when he actually went. So I sat with him, next to his bed, the music on, chilling everyone out, and I held one hand, his wife held the other and he slowly closed his eyes and slipped away.

I did district nursing from 1989 to 1999. I loved it, at the time. It was amazing. I couldn't do it now. It's so different now, it's all full of paperwork and targets and bollocks, basically. I like to be able to do things and help people.

CHAPTER SEVEN

Developing my career in the NHS

A few years later, I started to work in a NHS walk-in centre. It was the first nurse-led centre in the UK, at Boots the chemist in Birmingham. It meant the decisions on what to do with the patients, everything was all from nurses, not doctors or pharmacists, but nurses.

By this point I was a nurse practitioner, which is a senior nurse, not on a hospital ward. And while I was at this clinic, I did my first prescribing qualification which meant I could prescribe certain medication to patients – just like a doctor. I loved working there – it was a bit like district nursing because I was making the clinical decisions myself, and I was sort of in charge I suppose.

One day a patient said, 'My doctor is looking for a nurse to work in his GP surgery as a practice nurse.'

I was in the middle of taking his blood pressure, so I carried on regardless. Then, once I'd finished, I said, 'I'm happy here with this job, thanks all the same.'

'My doctor said, a car comes with the job, for whoever gets it.'

My ears pricked up at that. I thought oh, a car, wonderful, I could do with a new car, because I was running around in an old banger at that point, kept breaking down and costing me an arm and a leg in repairs.

So I took the details off the patient, I applied for the job and I got it. And the car of course!

That was when I started working with Dr Mohammed, the doctor who ripped me off for all the money. Turned out it would have been cheaper sticking with the old banger in the long run, but I didn't know that then.

This new Arab doctor started work too. The receptionist introduced us as it was the Arab doctor's first day. I happened to go into the doctor's room at the end of the morning and I said, 'How have you got on?'

He stared at me, looked me up and down. 'Oh my God, write your phone number down.'

'Why?'

'I've got to see you,'

'Really? Don't be daft.'

'Yes, really.'

So I wrote the number down on a bit of paper, as I stood up to leave.

He grabbed hold of me by the hand, pulled me close to him and kissed me, it was the most passionate kiss I've ever had – proper toe tingling, it lasted a while too.

While he kissed me he shook a bit, gasped and stopped kissing me.

'Are you all right?' I asked.

'No, I've had an accident. I've come in my pants.' He ran to the toilet and I'd never touched him. I swear to God I never touched him. I only kissed him. It must be my animal magnetism again.

I worked there for a few years, as the nurse in charge of this NHS clinic, and I started to do my own cosmetic work, and then Dr Mohammed asked me if I'd do some clients with him. And then all the debt started to mount up, and one thing and another.

I'd been working full time in the NHS off and on for more than thirty years. I was sad when I left the NHS – well, when I was made redundant by Dr Mohammed who was in charge of the clinic. He allegedly shut the business down and then reopened it under another name, and different company details – all perfectly legal – and he took all the other staff back on except me. He gave my job to another woman who wasn't even qualified to the same level.

I might sound a bit bitter about it, but honestly, I'm not. I enjoyed working there and I believe I gave the patients the best care I could. It was just so sudden – losing my job. And when I found out everyone else got their jobs back except me, that did hurt a bit. But I bounced back and got on with things. Plus, I was very busy in the middle of going bankrupt at the time, so I had bigger things to worry about. I knew I'd get another job and, sure as God made little apples, I did.

I used to do every Saturday and Sunday for one NHS walk-in centre for about two years and that was OK. And it was the scummiest place on this earth. It was two big Portakabins and the people who used to come in were rude, they used to throw food on the floor, the kids used to run around with snotty noses, and every now and then I'd have a blow out. I'd go into the waiting room and scream at people and then they all used to sit there and shut up for a bit. It was a funny old place, who knows how I stuck it for two years. But I made a lot of good friends, people I'm still friends with to this day.

But I think they were glad to see the back of me because the German guy Rudiger - don't mention the war - he was the senior GP in charge and he never asked me why I handed my notice in. I think he knew, and he was probably glad to see the back of me.

Why? You're probably wondering too. Well, it's because every Monday I used to ring Rudiger up and chew his ear off about all the things wrong while I'd worked the previous weekend. 'Right, do you know what, this weekend. We've got no sterile dressings... none of this, we've run out of the other.'

'Well that's not true, Mary,' he used to say. 'Because so and so said they stocked up on them last week.'

I knew that was shit, because I'd spent an hour running around trying to find some. 'Listen, there is none in that building and I'm absolutely appalled by it.'

He'd try and palm me off with another excuse or whatever.

I can be extremely stern, quite challenging and bossy, but I like that in myself. I think it's a good quality to have. I don't know if it's being a nurse that's made me like that, or if I was bossy anyway and so I'm suited to being a nurse.

I used to go into the waiting room at the GP practice and tell them all to shut up, that used to rile them like hell. There were signs on the ward, do not eat, do not smoke. They used to sit in the waiting room and throw paper bags, cartons and cups full of McDonalds burgers, chips, milkshakes on the floor. This was in

West Bromwich in Birmingham, which has a high proportion of black and Irish people and one thing and another. I'm pretty easy going but I do hate people that are disrespectful. When they used to throw things all over the place, it used to wind me up, so I used to throw the people out.

A few years ago, I went to a training course at the Royal College of Surgeons (RCS for short) in London about anatomy. It was called a cadaver course where they strip the skin back to show you all the blood vessels and veins and muscles. A cadaver is what they call a dead body used for medical teaching. Anyway, there were ten of us sat in rows in the room and as I walked in, I noticed this table at the front of the room. I thought, that'll be where the teacher stands, nothing unusual there. And then I noticed there's this lump on a silver tray in the middle of the table with this green fabric over the top. I stood there thinking, shit it's a head it's a head it's a head. I knew this because in the course instructions it told me we would be using a human head to illustrate what we learned about the body. That'll be the head, I thought.

The surgeon who was teaching us was Irish. He introduced himself, got us to go around the room and introduce ourselves, say why we were at the course. Then he stood behind the man's head and removed the piece of fabric. 'Right, ladies and gentleman,' he said. 'Now I want you to treat this man with the greatest of respect. He's eighty three years old and he's come all the way from America so that we can dissect his head.' As he pulled the cover back, I stared and, as predicted, it was just a head.

An old man's head, his eyes were open. I looked at the surgeon and I said, 'Does that mean we can't tell any Irish jokes?'

Fortunately everybody just laughed and it broke the ice, because everyone else was staring at the head and didn't know what to say.

The surgeon cut away parts of the head to show us blood vessels, and muscles, and one thing and another. A few of us at the back of the class room were talking about how much a head from America would cost. Somebody said £50 and someone else reckoned it would be thousands of pounds. Anyway, all this whispering behind me was getting a bit distracting so I put my hand up to ask a question.

'Yes, Mary, now what can I do for you?' the surgeon asked.

'There's a few of us wondering, how much does it cost for a cadaver head from America?'

'Now, here's the thing, so it's come all the way over from America, and we can use it for what we need to use it for.' He gestured to the head. 'And after a couple of weeks here, all we have to do when we're finished, is stitch it back up and return it to America so it can be buried with the rest of the kind man who's donated it.'

'Right, but how much does it cost?' I didn't know why but he seemed to be making a bit of a meal of it.

'Five hundred dollars.'

I thought that was pretty cheap, considering it had come all the way from America and had to go back there too once they'd finished. I wondered if there weren't any eighty three year olds' heads from the UK they could have used, but I didn't ask because I'd interrupted him enough and he was keen to get on pulling back the flaps of skin, showing us the nerves and muscles.

Before the course, we were shown around this very grand building, the Royal College of Surgeons, full of glass cabinets with old medical instruments and text books, and walls covered in paintings of significant surgeons of the day. An Indian professor at the RCS showed us around the building.

So we're moving from room to room, from painting to painting, and cabinet to cabinet, and Madge, the Indian professor, explained everything in the most frightfully wonderful posh English accent you've ever heard.

In the middle of the tour we were in this auditorium where they hold big lectures and events throughout the year. Madge explained they used to hold it for their elections and formal meetings of the college. He pointed to a mural painting on the wall from the 1800s. It showed various surgeons and scenes of them operating on patients. He pointed to one particular surgeon. 'Now this is interesting, here. This person was a woman but because they couldn't have women surgeons in a male industry, she spent her whole life pretending to be a man.'

'Err, professor, how did they know that she was a woman?' Everyone else stood in silence but I had to ask, because that's me, I have to know.

'Only when she died. They found out he was a woman pretending to be a man. She had a woman's body.'

'She must have really wanted to be a surgeon,' I said.

He nodded. 'Correct, Mary.'

'My God she had balls!'

'Correct, Mary, she had metaphorical balls but no real balls.' And he led us to the next room.

When I worked in another clinic in Birmingham, this little old lady came over to me. She used to come in regularly, sort of having an asthma attack and what have you. I treated her and I asked her how she was going to get home.

'I've got no money.' She put her hands in her pockets.

'Oh, don't worry, I'll take you home.' Anyway, I took her in my car to where she lived, bless her.

We arrived and she said, 'Will you come in now?'

'Look, love,' I said. 'I live bleedin' miles away from here. I've brought you home and you'll be all right now.'

She looked pretty sad – must have wanted some company for a cup of tea or something.

Next time she came into the clinic, she's gasping for air in the middle of an asthma attack. She found me said, 'Mary, Mary. It's all right, love, I've got a lift home tonight.'

Just in case it became a bit regular, I thought I'd better tell one of the doctors in the clinic. 'Look, I am insured, but I just wanted to let you know I have taken somebody home. I hope I did the right thing.'

'Well, you could've sent her in a taxi and claimed the money back.'

'What, from this fucking place? They wouldn't pay me. No, no, look, I wanted to take her home anyway.' I've got a soft spot for people like that and I wouldn't have left her to go in a taxi alone.

Once an Asian guy came into the clinic, he was so pissed. I mean I have never ever seen anybody so pissed. His eyes were red, he could hardly put a sentence together. Over the course of his visit, he explained he'd tried to go to his daughter's wedding, but she'd disowned him, which was why he'd drowned his sorrows I suppose.

I went over to see him and asked what he wanted help with but he'd wet himself and spilt food and booze and blood down his clothes from where he'd fallen over. I cleaned him up and I asked the other staff, 'Have we got a shower around here?'

'No,' everyone said, like I'd asked if we had a yacht or something.

'Oh, that's a shame.' Because it would have made cleaning him up much easier. So I sat talking to this man and asked him what he wanted.

'I want to go to hospital.'

'Trust me, they won't have you in hospital.' So I checked him all over and said, 'Look, you're fine. No reason for you to be in hospital. There's nothing wrong, you're just drunk. I've gotta get you back home. Have you got anybody to ring?'

'No, no.' He explained that he only lived round the corner.

'Look, I'm going to have to call the police to take you home.'

'No, no, no police.' He was quickly waving his hands at me and shaking his head.

'You'll be fine.' So I called the police and, not long after, these two coppers came in.

One woman police officer looked quite a religious fanatic, and the other – I couldn't work out if it was a man or a woman. I don't know even to this day.

The female copper said in front of the old man, 'He smells of piss, he's not going in my car.'

'Look, officer, you don't have to put him in the car, he actually only lives around the corner.'

She shrugged and waited for me to get the old man ready.

I cleaned the man up, handed him to the police and they took him off. I thought, at last, they've sorted it, I can get on and see to the other patients.

Half an hour later, the female copper stands in the middle of the clinic and says to me, 'He didn't live there.'

'Oh, I don't...'

I didn't really know what to say.

'So where is he?'

'Well you shouldn't have let him walk off on his own – he's so pissed he can hardly walk, let alone look after himself.'

'Yeah, if he comes back give us a ring.'

I couldn't believe it. I said, 'Give you a ring? You must be fucking joking.' I told them to leave because they were stopping me seeing other patients.

I got sick of all the aggro there. After I left, I thought I'd go to work for nursing agencies and do shifts in different walk-in centres and other places where they can use my nursing skills. And I've been doing that now, since 2012. It's great because I can fit it around the cosmetic/aesthetics work, it's flexible, and it's well paid. I do twelve to fifteen hours a week of nursing shifts through the agency now.

I love to do the NHS work alongside the cosmetics because I enjoy the variety. The NHS gave me my career, and I know it sounds a bit corny, but I like to give something back. And because I have got years of experience now, I couldn't just do this aesthetics alone, it would drive me mad. The reason is that people, or rather, some people, they whine so much. With the NHS, at least I can help them and make a difference from all my years' experience. I love the aesthetics too, but I wouldn't want to do one or the other full time. I'm happy to do a mixture, I like the variety. I love it in the NHS 'cos I can boss all these doctors around, and take the piss out of 'em, all sorts of things, it's wonderful.

Without the NHS skills I wouldn't have been able to do the cosmetics course – you had to be a doctor, dentist or a nurse prescriber to do the course on cosmetic procedures, so one led to the other.

At the moment on the agency I'm doing a job locally, a telephone job. They're paying me shed loads of money and I'm happy. It's a nice environment to work in. It's sort of helping people, giving them clinical advice over the phone basically.

This job means I can use my clinical knowledge as a nurse practitioner. I get them appointments, and prescribe over the phone. I have to wear a uniform because, if I don't wear it, I'm not the nurse. I don't feel like a nurse without the uniform. Nobody else does, everybody else wears what they want.

CHAPTER EIGHT

Working with homeless people

I worked with homeless people through an agency, off and on for eighteen months, for this Salvation Army homeless shelter. We used to give the homeless people a bed for the night, and a hot meal, and sometimes just somewhere they could be without the police moving them on or someone pissing on them while they slept – yes. that happened.

Someone asked me once if I'd been volunteering there, when I'd told them about a typical day. I said you've got no bloody chance, it was hard, dangerous, stressful work. Why on earth anyone would volunteer to do that sort of work, without being actually paid, is beyond me. In many ways, it was worse than working in a hospital with challenging patients, because we had none of the equipment or medical staff on site to help us, like we'd have done in a hospital.

This one day, one of the homeless men sort of tried to take advantage of me, sexually. It was really difficult. One minute he was stood next to me while I explained something to him, then he stepped closer, which made me feel a bit uncomfortable, but then suddenly he grabbed hold of me and pushed himself so he touched me. I could feel his erection against me and smell his bad, rotten-food smelling breath and sweaty body odour. Being as he was homeless, personal hygiene wasn't on the top of his list of priorities – but, unfortunately, trying to get off with me was.

He tried to kiss me and even thought I pulled my head away from him, he still managed to lick my cheek.

I pushed him off, told him to piss off and walked quickly away from him, the smell and the whole bloody thing really.

I went into the office and I said, 'Oh, I've just had an incident with this guy.' I didn't want to make a big thing of it, because it wasn't like he'd raped me, just a bit of a forced snog and a bit of a grope. I knew it could have been much worse.

'Oh, shall we put a yellow mark by his name on the system?' The manager looked up from the computer. The yellow mark would have shown to other workers there that he was a dangerous sexual predator and to watch themselves.

'No, no, no, can I deal with it?' I thought the yellow mark was going a bit far. By then I'd calmed down a bit and got it all into perspective – he hadn't hurt me, or even shown me his cock, but it was my pride that was hurt.

So next time he turned up, a while later – in the middle of the shelter, so everyone else could hear and see us – I grabbed his collar and I said, 'You fucking touch me again, Tom, and I will kill you.'

'Oh, I'm sorry, I'm sorry, I'm sorry.'

And, you know what, he didn't do it again.

I even had to resuscitate two people while I worked there. Heart attacks. We didn't have a crash trolley with the electric paddles to jump start someone's heart, like you have in hospital. I had to make the best of it with some mouth to mouth and pumping up and down on the chest with my hands.

The homeless people were on all sorts – legal highs, legal lows, all sorts of drugs, heroin, crack, ecstasy, marijuana, cocaine. The whole alphabet from A to Z.

I put up with a lot while I was there, because I needed to work, and I was used to people being challenging from my nursing days. But one day I thought, do you know what? I really can't do this anymore. That day I'd had a glass bottle thrown at me, narrowly missing my head as it smashed on the wall, another person had grabbed my bum when I'd turned around to hand him his bedding, I almost pricked myself with someone's needles and drug paraphernalia set he'd hidden under his coat, and the cherry on the cake was when I saw a guy with 'fuck off' tattooed around his mouth. 'So you haven't got a job then?' I said.

'No,' he said.

I came home that night thinking about all the crap I'd had to deal with that day, and thought, life's too short. I'll get another job somewhere else. So I never went back. It was sad in some ways, because among the horrible people, there were a lot of nice people, who'd thank me for helping, say how much they appreciated the food and bed for the night.

I was very empathetic, thanking my lucky stars I wasn't on the other side of the counter queueing up for a hot meal and a bed for the night, but some of them were just vile to me. I really needed to be paid danger money, but they weren't offering it, so I took myself off and got a job somewhere else.

CHAPTER NINE

Husband Number One

I've been married three times. I'm the Elizabeth Taylor of the West Midlands, only I didn't marry the same man twice. I've married three different men. Why? you're probably wondering. Well, I'm a romantic. I always believe the man I'm with is the one, and it sadly turns out he's not the one, he's a shit-bag or a cheat, or a boring bastard instead. But I'll tell you more about that later.

As a Libran, attractive and charming, men can find it hard to appreciate the intelligence and talents of a woman like me. Librans are also the most romantic of the star signs – we tend to have an idealised view of romance and tenderness and as soon as we fall in love, we think of marriage. That's me down to a tee.

I was nineteen when we got married. I remember going to the church together and the vicar said, 'Why do you want to get married here?'

'Because it'll look good on the photographs.' I'm not religious, I'm more spiritual and I didn't want to lie to a man of the cloth, so I just blurted it out without thinking, as I so often still do.

He nodded slowly. 'That's a good enough reason.'

Honestly, he did! Then we had to go to church for three months and we used to run in at the end of the service, to catch the last little bit to say we'd been there.

I can't remember Brian actually proposing to me. I think it was just we'd been together for a while and it seemed like the thing to do. In those days, it was all about getting married. People didn't live in sin like they do now. Isn't it funny how I still call it that? My kids just say they're living together without being married. I have plenty of friends who've been in a relationship and lived together for decades without being married. I'm old-fashioned. I think if you're in a serious relationship with someone you should commit and marry them, and then move in together. Maybe I wouldn't be divorced three times if I hadn't married Brian so young, but I'm still a great believer in marriage as an institution – even if it hasn't quite worked for me yet!

Brian was seven years older than me, which at nineteen was quite a big difference. I didn't know what to expect from being married. I was only just an adult. I knew how passionate and physical I was, even then, and I assumed Brian would be too. We got on well, had a laugh together, he was kind and thoughtful to me. I assumed that, in Brian, I'd found a man as passionate as me and that we'd live happily ever after together. But it was only once we were married that I realised how mismatched we were.

I met him when I worked at the university and he was a photographer. We used to go around photographing people's children and cats. I remember this one lady who said, 'Can you photograph my cat?'

'OK,' I said. This was the most photogenic pet ever, the lady asked us to take photo after photo of the bleedin' cat. I felt sorry for the poor animal, because the lady lived in a flat on the thirteenth floor. She kept this rabbit on the balcony and if the poor cat went out, for a bit of fresh air I suppose, the rabbit used to jump and shag it.

So, me and Brian met while we were photographing other people's cats and kids! We knew each other for a couple of years before we got together, and soon after we married, we bought a cottage together.

Like the cats and kids he photographed, he was sweet. He was also a lovely, kind, gentle man, but sometimes that's not what a woman wants, you know? He wouldn't hurt a fly, unlike another ex-husband of mine, but we won't go into that yet.

I'm a woman who likes a bit of adventure, who likes to have a laugh. I'm a very passionate woman – physical contact and sex are very important to me. So that's me, but as an example of what Brian was like, I remember once he was looking into my eyes as he was making love to me, and I said, 'What are you thinking about?'

He looked up from over my shoulder. 'I'm thinking about how many rolls of wallpaper it'll take to paper the walls.'

At that point I thought, this is fucking finished, you know. Anyone who's thinking about decorating the bedroom while he's making love to me isn't exactly living in the moment, enjoying the passion of sex with me. Although he was a nice guy, he was boring as shit, to be honest. He never wanted to go abroad on holiday – every year we had a fortnight in a caravan in Wales, just like when I was a kid. He didn't like eating out. 'It's a waste of money,' he would say.

'But I enjoy it. You like food,' I would reply.

'I think everything's a waste of money.' And the conversation would be closed once again.

I remember asking him one Friday night if he fancied going down the pub for a few drinks.

He looked at me like I'd just asked him to come to a lap dancing club. 'I'm going to creosote the shed.'

I used to like a bit of shopping on a Saturday and maybe grab a light lunch while I was in Birmingham. One Saturday morning I asked what he wanted to do. I said we could go into town, see what was on, maybe see a play at the Birmingham Rep theatre, go to one of the museums, see what photography exhibitions they had on. He used to love seeing other people's photos as it gave him inspiration for his own work.

'I need to go to B & Q for screws and paint.'

He was always painting or sanding something, or taking a door down and replacing it with another one, so I didn't ask why. I remember thinking I knew a screw I could do with and he couldn't get it in B & Q.

'Leave that,' I said. 'Come with me – we'll see some photos, see an early play, grab some lunch.'

'I've got to get on.' And he left the room tutting and saying something about buying a new hammer action drill.

When we married, we bought our first place in a suburb of Birmingham. It was a little cottage. When we bought it, the property was a semi-detached, and when we left, it was detached. We knocked through from the cottage next door making the two semi-detached homes into one, which we owned. It was a little white cottage with a thatched roof, like you see on the front of those posh biscuit tins. When we first moved in, and I'd just got married, it felt like I was living in my own little fairy tale. More fool me, eh?

The second home we had together was on the Lickey hills, a pretty little bungalow – on the edge of Birmingham.

To be fair to Brian, he was so useful when we moved into the house. He was very handy with the old DIY. We hardly had to pay for anyone to do the work – except the big bits of knocking walls through and putting in reinforcements so the house didn't fall down. All the rest – plastering, electrics, plumbing, decorating, Brian did it all. And he loved it.

He was never happier than when he was covered in building dust with a paint brush in one hand and a hammer in the other. He was my own Bob the Builder! The way he treated his tool box, I actually used to get jealous. He would always make sure the tools were clean and put them back in exactly the same place in the tool box, then put the tool box back in its place in the shed. I used to think if he gave me half as much attention in the bedroom, I'd have been a happy woman.

Because Brian was my first serious boyfriend, and my first husband, I didn't have much experience of sex and no other experience of what sex was meant to be like in a marriage. In those days people didn't talk about sex, not like nowadays where it's everywhere, and everyone talks about it online, and one thing and another. Then, you kept that part of your life private and didn't even talk to your friends. I wasn't unhappy with Brian – as I said, he was a kind, gentle man – but as the years went on, I realised there was something missing from my marriage. Though I didn't exactly sit about all the time worrying about it, there was plenty to keep me busy with setting up a new home, starting my nurse training, and getting to know the new neighbours.

There were two old ladies who lived next door to us and they were bloody hilarious; they definitely livened up what turned out to be a boring marriage! Hilda and Lilly used to cook on an open fire, and Lilly – she used to come round to borrow sugar and milk stuff like that – she looked like somebody had kicked her into a coal bucket and she'd never washed her face. It was ingrained with dirt and crap.

I remember this one occasion, we heard this banging clattering noise and Brian went round next door to see what was up. He put this ladder up to the bedroom window and he climbed inside, and he said, 'Are you all right?'

She was lying in her bed and said, 'What d'you want?'

'Well I heard this noise and I thought you wasn't very well or something.'

'I'm fine, I'm fine. Nothing to worry yourself about.'

He started to climb out the window, probably feeling a bit stupid for interrupting her.

She shouted, 'Brian, Brian!'

He climbed back up and popped his head through the window.

'Shut the door on the way out,' she said.

Another time, Lilly was lying there in bed with a torch reading.

A couple of burglars broke in downstairs, and ran up to her bedroom. They must have thought, this is going to be a doddle, an old dear in bed. They said, 'Where's your money?'

Lilly looked up from her book and shouted, 'In the TSB! Now leave me alone to my book!'

She told us all this after they'd left, and had just roughed up her kitchen a bit. They hadn't taken anything, but she rang us, and we came round to check if she was all right. We suggested she call the police.

She shook her head. 'They didn't take anything. Tidy up me kitchen on your way out. I just wanted you to know I'm still alive.'

We didn't call the police but we did give her kitchen the once over, cleaning up the mess the burglars had made.

It was sad in the end, because I remember when one of the old dears died. All the churchy people came round to me in my cottage and burst into song, singing Jesus Is Alive. And I'm standing there thinking, what the fuck is going on, who the hell are all these people, and what are they doing singing in my house? Never mind Jesus Is Alive, the old lady had died, and I thought they should have been paying her respects, not singing at the top of their voices.

I was married to my first husband for ten long years. When I say that to myself I wonder how I put up with it for so long when he was so boring, but like I said, he wouldn't hurt a fly and I'd got used to being with him. He wasn't horrible, so I didn't need to escape him, to run away because he'd hit me or anything. Nothing like that. But somehow I realised the life I had with Brian wasn't enough – not for me anyway. I know plenty of women who'd be more than grateful to have a man who was kind and nice and thoughtful, even if he bored you shitless, but not me. I wanted something more, I wanted more excitement, and I also wanted a passionate full sex life, which Brian wasn't interested in.

I wasn't really ever faithful to poor Brian. When I realised how uninterested he was in sex, I knew I'd have to get it elsewhere. And so I started to have little affairs here and there. Nothing serious really. A fling, I suppose I'd call them.

I was working in this elderly care unit and I was just about to hand over my patients as I finished my shift for the next lot to start theirs, when my mum rang me and I answered, 'Hello.'

'You're an absolute tart!' she said – no hello, how are you, or I need to tell you something – she was just straight in with the tart.

'Look, I'll call you back in a minute.' I put the phone down then went to the other end of the ward, called back and said, 'Don't you ever call me that again.'

'What's going on?'

I knew it would come out in the end because I'd been seeing a man called Flynn behind Brian's back for a while. This was a bit more than a fling really. It was a small community and people talk, people knew me, and who I was married to, so it was bound to come out. 'Well you know, I've left Brian.' I'd been thinking how I could tell my mum about it for a while and now she'd forced me to tell her. 'Look, I need to tell you something. I've actually been seeing somebody else.'

'Right, don't do anything until Wednesday when I see you.'

Like I could wait until then! I'd been thinking of leaving Brian for a while and I'd been seeing this other man for a bit too, so it was always going to end with me leaving. Anyway, that night at home I said to Brian, 'Look, I don't want to be married to you anymore.'

He didn't know what to say because he didn't know I'd been seeing someone else. He didn't know I hadn't been happy for a while, either, so it sort of came from nowhere as far as he was concerned. I suppose I should have told him I wasn't happy. But I'd tried with the passion and the sex and wanting him to do more interesting things with me. I'd tried when we'd first been married, and he never wanted to do it with me. So how long do you carry on trying something and expecting a different response? In the end, I gave up asking and rattled along on my own, doing my own thing.

Of course, he tried to persuade me to stay, said he'd change, said he didn't mind if I'd been seeing someone else, because he loved me, which was very sweet of him. In a way, it should have made me stay, but I ended up thinking he was being a bit of a doormat really, letting me cheat on him and not standing up for himself. Mind you, if he'd got angry about it, I'd have used that as an excuse to leave him. He was fighting a losing battle by that point. To be honest, my mind was made up – I was leaving him no matter what he said. I'd had enough and I wanted out of that marriage. I knew Brian wasn't as passionate as me, about life, love and everything, and I wanted to be with a man who was.

Me leaving Brian caused a lot of problems. But that was the end of Husband Number One.

At the end of the day, I thought I was making the right choice to leave him and start a new life with Flynn. I was sure Flynn was as passionate as me, that he'd give me everything Brian hadn't, which is why I jumped straight from the cottage with Brian into the arms of Flynn.

Flynn did give me my two beautiful children, and if I'd have stayed with Brian, I wouldn't have had any children, so there is that. But like most things in my life, it didn't run quite that smoothly. Flynn was passionate, and different from Brian in all ways possible but, as I found out, not everything about being different from Brian was quite as I hoped.

CHAPTER TEN

Husband Number Two

I met Flynn when he used to run the fruit and veg shop in the supermarket. Our eyes met over a cauliflower and half a pound of carrots! I felt something for him, because I wasn't getting that spark in my marriage at the time. Me and Flynn had a little bit of a fling while he was seeing this other girl. And I remember this girl's car parked at the back of where Flynn lived. And I did something terrible – I was so angry, I saw red – jealousy, anger, envy, the whole lot. I didn't think about what I was doing and I just poured a bottle of nail varnish all over her car and scratched all over the bodywork to bits.

I know now it didn't make sense. I was married and having an affair, so I couldn't talk because I was cheating on Brian, but for some reason I was so angry Flynn was still seeing this girl – I say girl because I think she was quite a bit younger than him.

I told him I didn't like him seeing this other woman. I said I'd left my husband and wanted us to be together. So he stopped seeing the girl and we decided we'd go for it – together as a couple, just us two.

I started to see Flynn, and my mum wasn't very happy about this. She thought I should never have left Brian, that Brian was a good, loving, kind man and why would I want to leave him?

Not long ago my mum said, 'I wish you'd have stayed with Brian. He was a lovely son-in-law and I'm sure he was a lovely husband to you.'

'You wouldn't have had any grandchildren if I had,' I said.

'Oh, yeah, maybe it was for the best you left him and had kids.'

'Exactly!' I replied, because I knew there was no answer to that.

After I left Brian, me and Flynn had to go and live with my mum and dad, which was sort of quite challenging. All of us squashed up in their little house, on top of each other. And all along, Mum didn't think I should be with Flynn. Dad didn't say much, because he never did, but I knew from his looks and when he said nothing what he thought. We got through it because me and Flynn were both really busy. We had the market business where we used to sell handbags and luggage and obviously I was a district nurse too. So I was always on the go!

However, my mum and dad hated him.

Me and Flynn had been together for a while and he wanted to get married, so we went to Mauritius for the wedding, which sounds so romantic and like something out of one of those brides' magazines. But he was bleedin' horrible.

We stayed in Mauritius for a few days either side of the wedding. Whenever I left his side he'd ask me where I was going.

'To the room,' I'd say.

'What for?'

'To get some sun cream. Want anything?'

'Stay here for a bit and then we'll both go together.' He smiled.

'I want to get my book too.' He'd been sitting in silence by the pool, so I wanted something to occupy myself.

He grabbed my arm and pulled me towards him. 'Sit down. I'll go to the room.'

I didn't want him rooting through my suitcase and my things so I said I needed to get something personal.

'What? It's our honeymoon. You should be spending it with me.' He pulled me back into my seat. 'Not sitting reading some bloody book, ignoring me.' He strode off to the room.

I was left rubbing my bruised arm and wondering what I'd let myself in for.

Later we were at a restaurant he'd picked, and when the waiter came to take our order I was about to give mine when Flynn interrupted. 'She doesn't know what she wants. She'll have the fish, same as me. And a bottle of white wine please.' He closed his menu and signalled to the waiter he was done.

When the waiter had left, I said, 'What'd you go and do that for? I wanted the chicken.'

'The fish is fresh from the sea. It says so on the restaurant menu. That's why we're eating here.'

I thought, no, the reason we're eating here is because you insisted we come here and wouldn't listen to where I wanted to bleedin' well eat, but I didn't think it was worth saying anything. 'The chicken looked nice.'

'What's the point of coming to the best fish restaurant in this area and ordering bloody chicken?' He folded his arms and leant back in his chair.

This was very different from how Brian would have been. To be fair to myself, it was very different from how Flynn had behaved when we were just seeing each other. But now he'd gone and married me, everything changed.

So the wedding and honeymoon in Mauritius was far from the wedding magazine bliss I'd imagined. By the time we were flying home, I sat next to him trying to read my book he'd not let me read during the holiday and he fell asleep. I managed a chapter or so until he woke up.

He took the book from me, closed it, then said, 'How much longer until we land?'

'I was reading that.'

'Not now you're not. You're talking to me.' Again with the same smile I would get used to seeing over the coming years. He had a glint in his eyes too. 'What do I want to talk to my new wife about?' He tapped his hands on his lap and then started talking about the market stall business and what he wanted my help with.

I reminded him I worked full time as a nurse.

'Love, honour, and obey, those were the vows. I want you to help me on the stall, so that's what you'll do.' And then he told me how he thought it would work, now we were working together as man and wife.

In a way, I suppose I could have coped with that, because if I didn't want to do things, I didn't bother telling him, I just didn't do it. But he was violent too. He had a terrible temper if I disagreed with him, which was why I didn't bother. His temper would flare if he'd had a bad day, or was frustrated with something, or someone didn't do what he wanted.

Once he was talking to Mum and she'd been trying to tell him how to do something with the business, or our house. Whatever, she was trying to give him some advice. She always wanted to help out, did Mum. It was well-meaning, she always was.

'I'll make up my own mind,' he said. 'I'm fine, thanks. I know what to do.'

Mum kept on trying to explain something to him.

'Fuck off, will you?' He pushed her onto the floor and ripped the ligaments in her arm.

I was screaming at him to stop. Mum was crying in pain. I couldn't believe what he'd done.

I called the police because I didn't know what else to do. 'My husband's assaulted my mum,' I told them.

The police came to take statements but nothing came of it. They said, 'It's a domestic.'

'My mum's arm ripped, I don't think so.'

'Nothing we can do.'

'A man assaults a woman in her 70s and you're telling me there's nothing you can do?' I couldn't believe it.

'If he does it again, let us know, then it will form part of a pattern. We have more chance of proceeding then.'

Flynn was a piece of shit, but he was my piece of shit who I was married to by that point, unfortunately.

Anyway, a year after the wedding in Mauritius, I fell pregnant and I had Joseph, my son. Flynn was OK with Joseph.

As a father, generally he was all right. He used to play with Joseph and buy him toys and take him out when he was old enough to be easier to look after. Flynn didn't do any of the nappy changing, feeding, or baby rearing, that was woman's work as far as he was concerned. He was a fun-time dad for Joseph. He took Joseph to the park, played football with him and he was always there if Joseph had hurt himself, or wanted to tell his daddy something, or ask him a question.

Five years later I fell pregnant with Kate, my daughter. When I was thirty eight weeks pregnant with her, Flynn hit me so badly, I had to go to hospital. He smashed me in the face. I crawled to the phone and called the police. The police took me to hospital but they said, 'Well actually, Madam, you hit him first.'

Which was true, I had, because he'd called me all these names under the sun – bitch this, cunt that, cow the other. I could only take so much, my emotions were all over the shop being so pregnant. I said to the police, 'Well don't you think I'm at a slight disadvantage? I'm thirty eight weeks pregnant, he's hit me in the face, bruised all down my face, and he's a foot taller and two foot wider than me.'

They didn't reply to that one. I suppose in an ideal world you shouldn't hit anyone, but in an ideal world a man shouldn't hit a woman, especially if she's pregnant with his baby. I was definitely not living in an ideal world at that point, I can tell you. I hit him with a walking stick because I couldn't walk properly, being as I was so pregnant. He turned round and smashed me in the face. It was shocking, honestly, because I'm not a violent person, I couldn't believe I'd done what I had, but he'd driven me to it. I also couldn't believe he'd hit me. It was like I was in a film of my life – looking down on myself from above. So I ended up in hospital for three weeks having Kate.

When I got home with the new baby girl, I was trying to get over being hit by Flynn, look after my baby and my little boy, and feed myself and my husband. It was a bit overwhelming to be honest. I remember that Christmas I'd bought Flynn some presents, doing my best between looking after the baby and Joseph as a toddler. I'd bought Flynn some bits while I was doing the weekly shop in Asda, wrapped them nicely, some clothes, something to open on Christmas Day.

He opened my presents to him. 'Why did you buy me stuff from Asda? George, these clothes are, that's Asda.'

I knew it wasn't designer, but it wasn't like I could pop out to Harrods or Harvey Nicholls, and this was before you could buy everything on the internet. I couldn't get out to buy Flynn anything, not with a baby and a toddler. I'd made do with where I'd already gone.

Some days I hardly knew who I was, between getting up and dressed, getting baby Kate up and washed and ready for the nursery, then making sure Joseph was ready for school and going off to work myself. I didn't know whether I was coming or going. I thought I'd done well – you know, actually making sure Flynn had some presents to open on Christmas Day, but no, that wasn't good enough.

I don't think he even bought me any presents. I remember him saying he'd given me the baby and wasn't that enough? He might have bought a pack of nappies 'cos he knew I'd need them, but nothing for me, not even some bubble bath or something.

After having Kate, I went straight back to work. Because I have to work – it's who I am. A few weeks afterwards, Kate was with a child minder in a nursery and I was back nursing and working on the market stall. I knew I wanted to provide for the two of them. By then Joseph was five, and walking about all over the place, asking for his mummy and daddy. I knew working would mean I could give them the things they wanted.

To be fair to him, Flynn always tried to be there for the kids but he was a terrible husband to me.

I stayed with him for fucking fifteen years and, now I look back on it honestly, who knows why? I suppose I stayed because of the kids, I thought it was better for them to have two parents who were together than split up. He was a good daddy to both of the kids. I saw how much he loved them, how much he enjoyed spending time with them, and how much they loved spending time with their dad too.

But then I thought in the end I just couldn't deal with how Flynn behaved towards me anymore. My marriage to Flynn is definitely a time I won't forget – not just for the two beautiful children we made together, but because how Flynn treated me has made me the strong person I am now.

When I think back to that time, it was probably one of the most difficult periods of my life. How did I deal with it? Honestly, when I think back to everything I was dealing with – bringing up two kids, working two jobs, running a house – I truly don't know how I did it. But that's me, I just carried on.

I get that strength from within, really. My mum and dad were very loving and very caring to me and the kids, so that saw us through the difficult times with Flynn. And I used to hide Flynn's behaviour towards me from the kids. I knew how much they loved him and didn't want them thinking any differently of him. So I never complained to Joseph or Kate about their father. I don't think that's right. I wanted them to make up their own minds about him, without me telling them what to think.

Not long before we got divorced, Flynn decided he was going to kill himself. 'I've had enough, I can't go on with this, with you anymore. I'm going to commit suicide.'

I called the police and explained I had reason to believe my husband was going to commit suicide and I couldn't stop him and so I needed someone round to help me so he didn't kill himself.

The police came and we found Flynn in the garage because that's where he was going to do it, but by then he'd decided not to kill himself.

Flynn sat on the chair in the garage, holding the rope in his hands and looking at the beam above his head where he reckoned he was going to string the rope up, and he said to the police, 'She shags young boys.'

I looked at the policeman. 'Look, I promise you I'm not a paedophile.' I had been having a fling with a much younger guy in his twenties. A while before this, Flynn had found out who it was, and went and battered the shit out of this poor lad.

The policeman looked from me to Flynn and back to me again. 'Looks like it's a domestic, and we'll leave you alone.' He left and, on his way out, grabbed me to say if my husband tried it again, to call them, but hopefully everything would be sorted now.

Sorted, I thought, not bleedin' likely!

A while later, one of my most vivid memories of Flynn is when we were on holiday abroad somewhere in Europe. The kids were throwing stones on the beach and building sand castles.

Flynn checked the kids were out of earshot and he said, 'I'm going to tell them what a fucking fat cunt and fat slut you are.' He thought I was having another affair with a young lad, but I wasn't at this point. I was just stuck with Flynn.

And in that second, I felt the anger build up inside me like a snake uncoiling itself until it lashed out and bit him. I got my fist and I hit him so hard I actually flattened him.

He fell onto his back and was rubbing his nose.

I stared down at him. 'You go and tell 'em.' I walked off and I think it was the best thing I've ever done. He drove me to it, you see. I'm not a violent person, but the way he spoke to me, the way he behaved with me, he made me into a violent person. I realised I had to get out of it all.

That was the straw that broke the camel's back. I thought, I can't and don't want to go on like this. I knew I wasn't happy because I'd had this fling with the younger man, and if I was happy in my marriage I'd never, ever do that – I believe in marriage, monogamy, the whole lot – but I wasn't getting what I needed from Flynn as a husband, so I looked to someone else for it.

I thought I'd found a man as passionate as me in Flynn. I thought I'd found someone who would give me all the love and excitement that Brian, my first husband, hadn't been able to. Only, the sort of passion I got from Flynn wasn't right either. Passion isn't anger or violence. I'd gone from a man with no emotions or fire in his belly to another man who had too much that spilled out and hurt me.

Anyway, after fifteen long, difficult years, I got rid of him. I'd tried to stay with him for the kids, and then realised I couldn't carry on being married to him any longer. We divorced. It was a period of my life and I've moved on from it.

My kids are simply fantastic. I had them with him, now I don't like him, and even today he doesn't like me, which is fine, because we don't need to like each other any more, but I've got two beautiful children to show for it.

I got rid of him, but I bloody well had to pay for it! I paid for the divorce, I paid him to go, and then he was supposed to pay me £200 a month for child support and I was paying £2,200 a month for the school fees, which I was managing to do. I always made sure the schools had their money because I didn't want the kids to have the same terrible experience at comprehensive schools as I'd had. I worked so hard to pay the kids' school fees every month – two jobs, nursing and cosmetics, I often did a 60 hour week – but I loved it.

Anyway, it turned out that, despite agreeing to the payments in the divorce settlement, Flynn never paid me any child support for eighteen months. He owed me three grand. Then my daughter Kate decided that she wanted to go and live with him and Flynn took me straight to the fucking Child Support Agency. They said I had to pay £258 a month for my daughter!

I rang the solicitor to ask if there was anything I could do because he owed me so much money.

'There's nothing you can do about it. If the CSA say you've got to pay, you've got to pay.' Absolutely shocking.

Alongside this, I was worried about how the divorce would affect the children. Joseph was about fourteen and Kate was about nine when we divorced. I'd explained to them Mummy and Daddy weren't going to live together any more.

'What's gonna happen to the cats?' Kate asked, crying.

'We're keeping them,' I said. 'And we're staying in this house.'

Joseph was made up, because he got to keep his bedroom and would still see his dad at weekends and do all the fun stuff with him, and none of the boring homework and being told off stuff that I had to do with him.

Kate shrugged, grabbed the cat and said, 'Well, that's all right then.'

I actually had my first breakdown when I was married to Flynn. I thought I'd never get over it, I thought I was going mad. I wanted to hang myself. I didn't want to die, but I knew I didn't want to be living my life, or be myself. It's amazing what people can cope with and I did.

Flynn used to accuse me of all sorts of rubbish – shagging young boys, finding a pubic hair in the soap was evidence that I'd shagged the neighbour, he even noticed some hand prints on the boot of my car and said I'd been shagging someone in the car. All lies, all made up, all shouted at me at top volume and usually followed by a slap or a punch in the face. No wonder I had a nervous breakdown, but any more of that's not for now, I'll come back to that, don't you worry.

CHAPTER ELEVEN

Having children - Joseph

Private education? Some people argue for it and some people argue against it, but as far as I'm concerned, it's the best thing you can give your children. It's money well spent, in my book. My kids are both exceptionally sociable, they've had a brilliant start in life. The private education has paid off for them because my son, he's laughing all the way to the bloody bank, he's an investment banker now. My daughter is at university at the moment studying geography, she wants to be a weather presenter.

I just wanted to give them the best that I could, which is why I put them both through private schooling for most of their lives. I wanted my kids to have the opportunities, which would lead them to a life more interesting and full of more chances than my parents' lives had had, and more than mine. I felt private education was the best way to do that. I would say my greatest achievement outside of work is definitely my children.

Becoming a mother for the first time was lovely, but I was sort of back at work in no time. I'm a workaholic and I had to get back to work – I am my work, I think. I'm happy when I'm working, so why would I want to give that up because I'd had children?

Although becoming a mother was wonderful, the actual birth of my son, Joseph, was fucking horrendous. It was a difficult pregnancy, probably because it was my first. I worked until I was twenty eight weeks pregnant and then I couldn't work anymore. I had lots of sickness, couldn't eat, couldn't keep any food down, so I stopped working. I went into Worcester Hospital and they put these things inside me to induce me into labour, which wasn't the nicest of experiences. Then my waters broke and I had to lie there with the worst midwife in the world.

She was running around saying, 'Oh god, we've got to do this at such an early time in the morning, this is terrible!'

Everything I needed was too much bother, or she'd run off throwing her hands in the air, like I'd asked for a foot massage and some silk sheets. Having been a nurse at that point for many years, I can tell you, the official term for her bedside manner was shit.

Then the midwife put a size 22 catheter into me, which was far too large and so it was really painful. I remember the bag hanging over the side of the bed full of blood as well as my own piss. And the midwife did nothing about it. I was too out of it to complain at the time, but afterwards I wanted to. But by the time I'd got home I didn't want to think about it anymore.

She made me feel terrible. I was absolutely terrified.

The doctor told me I had to have a caesarian, so I thought, OK, that's what I'll have, no panic there.

But the midwife kept running around and saying, 'Oh god, it's the worst time to have a caesarian! It's going to be terrible, I don't know why you're having one now!'

Like I had a choice about when I was having the caesarian! She wasn't exactly calming me down.

I had my son under epidural, so at the time I didn't feel anything, but afterwards, that's when the pain hit me like a train. He came out looking so beautiful so it was worth all the hard work.

Afterwards I was so swollen up and in pain I'd never felt agony like that before, and never did again until I had my daughter years later. I had a Caesarian and I watched it all happening under the big theatre lights and it was so bloody terrible. It only took about half an hour from start to finish but I lay there, watching them cut me open, reach in and eventually remove my son from my body, all under the theatre lights. It felt quite surreal, like it wasn't me they were doing it to.

When I saw them cutting me from hip to hip across my stomach and pulling my tummy open, I thought, oh my god, I'm going to be really sore afterwards. They put the clips in to hold my stomach together after they sewed me up, and then five days later the clips came out and I was discharged. Suddenly I was shopping with a baby in a pram and a bloody sore stomach still.

Luckily after all this trauma, Joseph was fit and well and wonderful. He was born in the third week of December and I came out five days later. I can't remember much about being in hospital, except the pain and being handed my baby son, and how my husband hardly came to visit me.

My son's very bright, but at the same time he can also be very thick. We had him going for ages with this wind up when he was six to eight years old. We told him that on this beach in Wales there were currency shells. We put some money in these shells, you see.

'Oh my god, this is brilliant! Money!' he used to say, and he would run around on the beach, going demented trying to find the shells. Some of 'em had fifty pence inside and some of 'em had a pound. He used to run back to us on the beach, clutching the coins he'd found, and say, 'Look what I got, I wonder how many more I can find today!' And off he'd go, running around trying to find the shells with the coins inside – the special currency shells we used to call them.

When Joseph went to school for the first time it was so emotional. To see him in his little shorts and little polo shirt was wonderful. I didn't get upset, like some mums do, I felt so proud that he was starting school, and hopeful he'd have a better time at school than I had.

Joseph had been at a state primary school for a few years and the teachers picked him out and realised he was very bright. When he was seven, his reading age was eleven and a half. The sad thing was, they couldn't do anything with him – they used to give him the people that were underachievers to look after. He could do it all with his eyes closed, he was so bored, they said.

I wanted him to strive and live an interesting life, more than what I'd managed. So I approached a private school not far from me, and they were really keen to have him.

The head mistress said, 'Your son is exactly the sort of pupil we encourage to attend this school.'

To me, it was just so important for him to have the opportunities I'd missed because I ended up in a bloody comprehensive school. I took him out of the state primary school and Joseph went to private school from seven years old.

With my daughter, I managed to put her into private school when I started doing the Botox. It enabled me to send her as well from when she was about eight.

The private schools were absolutely brilliant – they taught them so much academically and wider than that – about communication, confidence, everything you need in the real world.

When they were quite young, Joseph made a badge for Kate to wear at their school that said, I am a girl, not a boy. Because everybody kept thinking she was a boy because of the way she looked, with short hair and not being developed at that age. She soon caught up, though!

Joseph's school had this auction and I remember putting in a prize of Botox and a chemical facial peel and nobody had bid for it. They didn't want people to know they would have cosmetic procedures, which was quite funny, because I was looking at them thinking: My god, you've had it, you've had it too. Maybe you need it. You could definitely do with a bit of help.

They were at that school until they turned thirteen, then they went to another school afterwards. My son went to Monmouth from thirteen onwards.

After he'd aced the entrance exam, they were so overwhelmed and keen to get him into their school they said, 'Madam, we can offer you thirty per cent off.'

I thought about it for a bit, because it was still pretty expensive. 'No, no, I can't afford that.'

'How about forty per cent off?' Because they really wanted him to go there.

'Yeah, yeah, I can afford that.' I remember thinking, I might not be able to afford that at the moment, but a few more cosmetic procedures and some NHS shifts and it'll all be fine. It cost about as much as a decent second hand car - think it was about £6,000 a year and he was boarding – but I knew I wanted to spend it on him, and bugger the bloody car. I managed with some old banger, because who cares about a car when you can give your kids the gift of education? That's how I thought about it anyway.

Joseph was very competitive at school, and an exceptionally good runner. He took part in the under thirteens. He had a race with this lad and Joseph beat him by quite a long way. At the final, which was held at Birchfield Harriers, he ran a race and won a gold medal which the Lord Mayor presented to him. It was such a proud moment, as his mum who'd brought him up, to see him doing so well as a teenager. He was very athletic and very sporty. He still is now.

I used to go to the private school, for teachers evening. I'd get all dressed up like the other parents.

Joseph would grab me after I'd seen a few of his teachers with him. 'Will you stop treating my teachers like they're your mates?'

'What do you mean?' Because I'm friendly with everyone, it's just how I am. I'm always putting my hands on people's shoulders, offering to help them.

'They're not your mates.'

'Yes, they are.'

'You're too familiar with them. It's mortifying, Mum.'

I knew what he meant, because earlier that night I'd gone up to one of his teachers and said, 'What's your name?'

'What do you mean?' this teacher said.

'You're Billy No Mates.'

'Why?' the teacher asked.

'Well, you got nobody here, wanting to talk to you. Tell you what, I'll come and talk to you.'

Joseph was absolutely mortified at his mum behaving like that.

When he turned seventeen he passed his driving test and I bought him this car, but I thought I'd have a bit of a wind up with him about it first. I parked this Fiat Brava on the drive and I brought him home and I said, 'Oh for God's sake, who's bloody put that on the drive? Some idiot's parked that on our drive.'

'Typical, idiots parking on our property,' he said, shaking his head.

I left it a few moments, then I handed him the log book and keys from my handbag.

He actually cried, and Joseph doesn't cry, he's not a crier. 'Is it mine?'

'Well it's not for me, I've already got my own. 'Course it's for you!' I'd asked the school if it was OK for him to have a car and use it to drive to and from school.

'Yeah, you can take it, he can use it, but he's not to take any friends.' And then the teacher laid down all these other rules and I was just ignoring it.

The first weekend he had it, Joseph took the car somewhere and then I don't know what him and his mates had been doing, but they all decided to jump all over this girl's car from his school and cause all this damage. They dented the girl's car by jumping on the bonnet and roof. Like I say, fuck knows what they were thinking – not much probably.

So I got a phone call from the girl's dad saying what was I going to do, with my son causing all that damage, and if I didn't pay up he'd call the bloody police. That phone call cost me £1,250.

During the same bloody week, Joseph wasn't supposed to take anybody in his car, and he ended up hitting a man's car.

The owner of the other car rang me and told me about the damage, a bumper and a scratched front wing, he reckoned.

'Look, I don't want it to go through the insurance, it's going to make his premium go through the roof, and it's already nearly as much as the car's worth. I'll pay for the damage he's done to your car.' Which ended up being £500, so that wasn't too bad. We'd agreed on that.

A couple of days later, this guy rang up and said, 'I'm just taking my car to the garage and I'd like to have the alloy wheels redone, and I could do with replacing the back bumper as well, and the clutch is on its way out. Basically, it's going to be a bit more than we said.'

I couldn't believe the cheek of the man. 'Look mate, do you want me to buy you bleedin' dinner as well? Look, piss off, you're having that done, to fix the damage my son's done to your car, and don't take the piss out of me.' I put the phone down.

So that one week Joseph actually cost me about £1,700. But apparently I never do anything for my kids, they reckon!

A few weeks later, I remember we were in his car, Joseph driving, and all of a sudden he hit this rabbit. He stopped the car and started running up the road.

'What you doing?' I shouted out the window.

'I've gotta photograph the first rabbit I ever hit!' But obviously the rabbit had run off.

In comparison to the state school, the private school was more strict. I noticed how much more regimented Joseph's timetable was and how it opened up a whole new world of opportunities for him. It was just incredible actually, because they allowed him to fulfil what he was capable of, to challenge him, to stretch him, if that makes sense.

As soon as he left Monmouth he got himself an internship at Rothschild's, and they actually paid him, which is quite rare because most internships you have to pay them to be there, he explained. I think he was paid £20,000 for six months to work for them. He put the money to one side rather than just splashing it about; he's very astute with money, is Joseph. Then he went off to Thailand to teach kids sport for another six months.

I think the private schools have given him the confidence to just go off and do things like that, without worrying, to just live a rich fulfilling and interesting life.

Now, he's a very confident and opinionated man.

I said, 'Oh I'm writing a book.'

'Yeah.' He shook his head at me, as if to say, yeah right, whatever Mum.

'I'm calling it Confessions of a Botox Babe.'

Without a second's pause, he replied, 'I think you should change the title.'

'No, I think you should mind your own business because that's what it's gonna be called!'

'Oh. OK.'

'I am the Botox Babe, and that's what it's about.'

'All right Mum,' he said.

If I had to give him advice on his wedding day I'd just tell him to enjoy it. I've been married three times, so I know a thing or two about marriages and wedding days. I'm sure there's gonna be a fourth husband soon enough.

I believe in the whole institution of marriage, the diamond rings, the ceremony, everything. I said to my son, 'You know what, if you're going to get engaged to your girlfriend, I've got some diamonds in my old wedding rings.'

'Shut up.' He screwed his face up.

'OK, OK. Maybe not then, but they're there if you need 'em!'

I hope my children will get married and live happily ever after, but who knows?

CHAPTER TWELVE

Having children - Kate

When I had Kate, I was convinced that she was going to have either Down's syndrome, or something else wrong with her. I was on that many drugs, I couldn't bloody walk. Flynn had hit me so badly that I ended up in hospital at thirty eight weeks pregnant and I was in there for three weeks having Kate.

When Kate was born, I was under a general anaesthetic. She came out and was crying real tears.

My mum said, 'I'm not surprised, with what you've been through, Mary.' She was so angry that Flynn had hit me while I was carrying his child.

Talk about put your foot in it – my daughter was a nightmare!

I remember buying their grandmother a fake Rolex watch, and I said to Kate, 'Now look, don't tell your nan what it costs.'

And she walked straight in to see her nan and she said, 'Here's your present Nan, it only cost a fiver.'

I couldn't believe she'd said it.

She looked at me with her big eyes, blinking like a cartoon character. 'I thought you told me to tell her.'

I shook my head. 'No!' She can't keep her mouth shut when it needs to be kept shut.

More recently, when I was selling the house next door, I would be showing the people around, explaining all the good features the house had.

She'd clatter down stairs from her bedroom and say to people, 'Oh, did mum tell you about the rat?'

And I was like, oh here we go again, trying to make a cutting motion with my hand across my neck.

She carried on, regardless, chatting away. 'There was this rat outside, and we threw this piece of bread and it took it and went back to its nest.'

And the people are, like, backing out the house. 'I think we'll leave you to it.'

After the people viewing the house had gone, I said to Kate, 'What'd you do that for?'

'Well it happened!' She stood with her hands on her hips and her big innocent wide eyes staring at me, like butter wouldn't melt.

'Yeah, but don't bloody tell people if they're coming to maybe buy the house.'

'Oh well!' she said, and ran off to cause mayhem somewhere else.

When she was a little girl we'd all gone to the cinema. 'Right I've just cleaned the car, so don't make a mess.' I opened the back door for her to get in.

She tripped over the edge of the car and threw the whole paper bucket of popcorn, about the size of her head, into the back of the car, all over the seats, floor and under the front seats.

'What you done that for?'

'I didn't mean to.' Again with the big brown eyes blinking at me.

There was no way I could tell her off. I've never been able to tell her off really.

She's actually got a condition which was only identified in the sixties. It's something called hyperlexia, and it means that she's sort of thinks faster than her brain can work. It's the opposite of dyslexia they told us. I sent her to this psychologist woman and it came out that she'd got this hyperlexia.

It cost me three hundred quid, but it was worth a fortune for her, because she then got a free computer, free printer, loads of extra tuition at university. Her brain is thinking faster than her body can keep up with.

Kate is just Kate, she's just an absolute bloody nightmare. She's just really funny and she's a Gemini so she's energetic, clever, adaptable, witty, and she tends to react so a situation instantly, without thinking first.

She had to look after the school guinea pig when she was a little girl. She brought it home in a cage and said, 'Mummy, we've got to look after it for the Easter holiday. We must look after it very well.'

I wouldn't have it in the house, horrible little thing, it looked like a bloody rat.

'The other girls and boys put it in their kitchen,' she said, putting it on the kitchen table.

'Don't be silly, it goes outside.' I put it on an outdoor table round the back of the house, next to the back door.

The morning after I went outside to check on the guinea pig and something – a fox maybe – had rolled up the wire and eaten the guinea pig. Whatever it was had only left about three tufts of hair. I thought, oh shit, it's gone.

Kate stood, staring at the empty cage and the little tufts of hair. 'I told you we should have kept it in the kitchen.' She shook her head. 'I don't want to get into trouble, Mummy.'

'No, no, it's all right,' I said. So I phoned up the school and said, 'I'm ever so sorry but the guinea pig's gone.' I thought, there's no point beating around the bush, just get out straight away what's happened.

'Is the cage OK?' the teacher asked.

'Yes.' I mean, except the wire which was rolled up, but I thought, I'll be able to roll that back down, no bother.

'That's fine then. Bring the cage back when Kate returns to school please.'

Bloody clever fox though, whatever it was, rolling up the wire netting!

Kate is a nightmare, but I love her because she's my daughter. She's hard to please, high maintenance, demanding, a bit of a princess at times, but that's how she is and that's how I love her to be. She's brutally honest too; just like me. I can't bear it when people fanny about not getting their words out, not saying what bloody well needs to be said. Cut to the chase, say it, and move on!

I bought Kate a car, about £4,200 I paid for it and at the time I was driving round in a fricking £450 Ford KA. I'll do anything I can for her and her brother.

I see her about every two or three weeks. My daughter the other week said, 'Oh, I've got no money, I've got no money!'

'Well, if you come home I'll give you £400.'

'I'll come home tonight, Mum.' And she did, she was straight back like a homing pigeon that night to see me.

She and her brother both live in London, so I can't see them that often, but we talk on the phone every week. She's very beautiful, very photogenic. She's very much like me, spending money like it doesn't matter – she likes to enjoy her money, same as me. Kate tries to be careful with money then she'll call me and say she's run out, and doesn't know where it's all gone! The son is as tight as a duck's arse, like his father.

Kate's been to private school since nine years of age. I wanted her to have the same opportunities that Joseph had had at that age. Mind you, at one stage I tried to persuade her to go to a state school, I was trying to economise or something and another.

She freaked out and said, 'I'm not bloody well going there.' So she stayed at the private school right the way through until she left after doing her A levels.

It was definitely money well spent because but it's stood her in good stead. Now she's at university studying geography, doing really well, with plans to be a weather presenter on TV. And she's that determined, I'm sure she'll do it.

My daughter is very creative and she's exceptionally beautiful, she really is. She made me a book of memories and photos from holidays we had together, her childhood, all sorts. It was so beautiful, photos, ticket stubs, brochures from places we'd been, all stuck in and she decorated them with ribbons and bound it into a beautiful book.

Now my children aren't children any more, I can see how different they are. Joseph is very academic and sporty – Kate is very creative and bubbly.

A few years ago, I remember me and the kids, we went to St Kitts – one of my patients used to live six months in St Kitts, and six months in England, and she told me how wonderful it was, so I thought let's book a holiday and see what it's like.

We went out there to stay with this client and we spent nearly every day together. They had an enormous Marriott hotel golf course that went on for miles. We could have played golf all day every day and not got bored, it was that big. Me and Kate crashed the golfing trolley into trees because we were laughing so much and distracting each other. Joseph was teeing off, playing golf really serious like.

We went away for two weeks and I couldn't get them out in the evenings. We went out two nights and they fell asleep both times!

'Come on let's go out!' I'd say.

'Oh no, Mum, we're tired.' Or 'Maybe tomorrow night, leave us alone.'

They know I'm me and that I like a good party and a dance and a drink. They should have expected me to be making them go out on holiday. I expected them to want to join me, since they're quite a lot younger. You know what they say, youth is wasted on the young!

A while ago, Kate and I went to Croatia. I drove into Zagreb, minding my own business.

All of a sudden, Kate's shouting, 'Mum, there's people looking at you.'

'I know, love. I've stayed in that hotel over there but I actually shouldn't be here on this bit of the road.'

'Well, he's looking at you.' She pointed to a man in uniform.

Our car was stopped on the tramlines, this whistle blew, and a police officer walked up to the side of the car.

I just put the window down, calmly because I knew he wasn't going to shoot me or anything, and I put on my very posh English accent and said, 'I'm so sorry officer, I'm English and I don't know what I'm doing.'

'Oh, don't worry, Madam, just go round the corner.' He pointed to where I was meant to stop the car.

Every time we came to that corner, I did it again. I did it three times in three days. They must have thought, oh god, it's this bloody mad English woman again!

Eventually we arrived at this hotel and a nice young lad greeted us at the front entrance and said, 'Can I take your cases?'

I thought, this is nice, you know, five star treatment, I could get used to this. Anyway, we got into the reception with my trolley dolly wheelie suitcase with the handle that packs away when it's not being used, you know the one. Well anyway, the handle was a bit dodgy and when this young lad picked it up, the handle fell off.

Of course, Kate's been watching the whole thing, like a Russian spy or something. 'Oh Mum, he's broken your case.'

'Oh my god! He has!'

And this poor young lad's face was going redder and redder. He was trying to put the handle back into the case but it kept falling off.

'My mum doesn't care,' Kate said.

'I bloody well do,' I said. 'That case was from Harvey Nichols; it's designer, Gucci, or Pierre Cardin, or something or other.' Because it was, something like that anyway, and I remember it had cost a pretty penny when I bought it.

The poor young lad looked at me, the broken handle in his hands, and a sad expression on his face.

'Look here, you,' I said. 'You're going to have to take us out to dinner tonight.'

Kate was egging it all on, making more a deal of it than it really was, saying how upset I was, and one thing and another. So we agreed he'd take me out for dinner that night as an apology.

The next night, Kate wouldn't bloody well go out with me and the lad. She refused to leave the room, said she felt embarrassed and didn't really mean for him to take us out for a meal.

'Well, it's a bit bloody late for that,' I said. 'You should've kept your bleedin' mouth shut before.'

In the end, I paid for our dinner, because the hotel staff out there aren't very well paid and it seemed a bit harsh for him to pay a week's wages for a meal with me. We had a lovely meal together, he told me all about working at the hotel, his family in Zagreb and how he'd come to work at the hotel. Of course, I had quite a lot of wine – as usual, and he had to bring me back to the hotel staggering and swaying a bit side to side. I think at one point I was even singing – Ave Maria or something.

The lad told me his name was Avare, and every time I go to Zagreb I ring him up and we go out for a drink – catch up on what we've been up to. He tells me if he's had any other mad English women like me and Kate; if he's broken any other expensive suitcases, that sort of thing.

That little set up is Kate all over – stirring things up for her own amusement, and then ducking out when it gets too much for her. She's very mischievous, but I wouldn't have her any other way, I love her to bits.

I didn't really have any difficulties raising my two children; I suppose I just got on with it, between working and looking after the family. Sometimes it was difficult, with work and one thing and another to find time for the children, but I did manage to spend time with them – I made time to be with them. It wasn't difficult to actually bring them up, to have children, because I just gave them what they wanted really, the best sort of education, and plenty of love and fun times with me.

Yeah, they were spoilt, they are spoilt now still, but fuck it, they're my kids and I'll spoil them if I want to. Without doubt, the most rewarding thing in my life is seeing Joseph and Kate achieve their goals in life – watching them become the adults they want to become, live their lives how they want to live them. Having the private education gave them so much, and it's paid off now because they're both flying with their own lives.

If I had to do it all again, raising my two children, I wouldn't do it any differently. I've ended up with two very successful driven young adults, and I don't regret anything. And now they're grown up, I've got a lovely relationship with them. Sometimes! My son and daughter, they're my life really, that's why I'm such a fucking workaholic I just keep going and going and going for me, and for them.

CHAPTER THIRTEEN

Training to be a Botox Babe

Even though I ended up bankrupt from doing the cosmetic procedures, it's given me so much: tuition fees for my children, free surgery for me, a very lucrative business of my own.

It all started because I needed the money to send Kate to private school, just like Joseph. It didn't seem right to send one and not the other. I couldn't afford both on my nurse's wages, so through a friend of a friend I found out about Botox, and it all came from there.

Because I wasn't able to go to private school, I wanted to strive so my kids could. In the same way I wanted to live a life that was more interesting than my parents', I wanted my kids to live a rich, exciting life full of opportunities. And the best way to start them on that road was to put them both through private school. And private school needs money, and that was where the Botox came in so handy to pay for it.

During one week a few years ago, I banked £15,000 in fees for the cosmetic work. This was when a full time nurse in the NHS earned about £25,000 a year, so I couldn't believe it. I felt like some sort of cosmetic procedures celebrity.

When I started doing it in 2003 I was right in at the beginning – not many others were doing Botox and fillers. It's not like it is now on the TV, with everyone with perfect white teeth, smooth foreheads and plump lips – people didn't know about what you could have done without touching a surgeon's knife, and how it could all be quite affordable, like having a haircut, getting fake tan or a tattoo done.

I'm very lucky I've been doing this these Botox injections since then, and I've still got customers that were with me at the beginning, so I must be doing something right. Every couple of weeks I get new customers.

I was very lucky, because after going on the training course, I started doing the procedures and did more and more until it was almost another full time job. I've been told I'm very good at what I do, to be honest, so people like the fact that I smile and have a good bedside manner. Also, I like to bring in my nursing experience to give my aesthetics customers a better, more holistic experience with me, whether it's on the phone for a consultation or in person at my home clinic or in one of the clinics where I work.

For those of you who don't know how it works, cosmetic procedures are very much like any other sort of medical consultation. I get a phone call to find out what they're wanting me to do, and from that I can get a feeling of whether I want to work with that client or not.

In an average week, I probably work about thirty or so hours on cosmetics work including phone calls, consultations, ordering, procedures. I have enough work to turn people away if I don't think I'll be able to work with them. I get a feeling in my gut on the phone call. If they're rude, I just tell them to try someone else. I was in the car and somebody phoned up and said in a really strong Brummie accent, 'D'yaw do Botox?'

'Hello, my name's Mary, and who have I got the pleasure of speaking to?'

'Me name's' whatever it was, she said. 'D'yaw do Botox?'

'Darling, where would you like it, in your vagina? And your arms? In your head?'

'No, no. I want me eyes doing.'

And I was thinking, really, really, OK, because normally I'd see the client and discuss where on the face would have the best results from having Botox.

'How much?' she asked.

'For you, it would be over two hundred pounds.'

She huffed. 'Well, I can get it for £150. How comes you're so dear?'

I thought, I've wasted enough time on this rude woman. 'Do

you know what darling, fuck off and don't ever ring me again! Don't ever insult me and my services.' I put the phone down, and guess what, she never rang me back! You want something cheap, that's fine but don't tell me you can get it somewhere else. You're not comparing my service with some back street dodgy one. You know I'm not interested in having to defend my very reasonable prices.

Anyway, as long as I've not put the phone down on them, and once I'm happy I can fit the client in, and I'm going to be able to work with them, I meet the client. If they're a regular customer, I know them anyway. I see the customer wherever is best for them – my home clinic, or one of the other ones where I work around the country. When I see the customer face to face I do an assessment, to work out what they are wanting to be done, and whether that's suitable for their body. Also if they have any underlying health conditions and whether they've had any procedures done before.

Especially if it's somebody new, I give them the information about what the procedure involves, explain if it hurts, how much it hurts, all that sort of thing, so they can go away and decide for themselves.

I don't do any procedures I've not already had on myself, so I can give clients an honest description of what it feels like.

I talk about their general health, what their expectations are, if it's possible, that sort of thing. Because of my training in the NHS and because I still work within the NHS, I've got a lot of wider clinical knowledge. So a lot of people like to pick my brains. I'm happy for them to use my knowledge like that.

I'm absolutely confidential with people, if they're asking about all sorts of aspects of health. I'll pick up on things wider than just cosmetics, like if somebody's got a mole on their face, so I measure it and write it down and say, 'If that ever changes, you need to go to your doctor because it may develop into skin cancer.'

It's not like I can stop being a nurse just because I'm giving someone a consultation about Botox injections. I am a nurse, and I'll always be a nurse until the day I die.

When I see the patients, that's when I like to discuss prices. I have a menu card of prices and procedures, a bit like when you go to the hairdressers. I keep my prices reasonable and haven't put them up since 2003, although I do believe you get what you pay for.

Then I order the products for them – the Botox or the fillers or whatever it is they're having done. Then they have a cooling off period in case they decide they don't want to go ahead. Even if I've ordered the products, they can still change their mind. I don't want any customers having anything done they're not one hundred percent going to be happy with. It's not compulsory, any of these procedures. It's a big decision, especially if it's the first time someone's having anything done. Having the cooling off period works really well for me and the clients.

I do facial peels. These are just like it sounds, it peels off your skin. I apply the product onto the face, and three days later the face sort of peels off. Basically, it takes off the top layer of your skin and the skin underneath is all sort of new and rejuvenated, like getting a new face. And it takes about a week to go through the process but the skin is glowing afterwards. You can do it on the décolletage and the hands as well. The results are really good and people are generally very pleased with it. It's a bit warm, it's not painful and when it peels off it's a bit irritating, because your skin peels off, but that just means it's doing its work right. A lot of my clients come back and have another one because they're so happy with the results.

There's a lot been said in the media about Botox and the dangers, and why you shouldn't have it. I honestly swear by it. It's my most popular procedure by a long way.

The results after the Botox injection are so visible and clear, it's just almost like magic. It removes all the wrinkles in the forehead and around the eyes – leaving the face completely smooth.

There was one guy, and after I injected him he looked at the photograph I'd taken before the procedure. He must have had some sort of head injury and it wasn't until I looked at the photograph and I'd injected him, we noticed it had completely taken the effects of the injury away. I looked at the before photographs, and I thought, bloody hell, he's got half his muscles missing. And I actually said, 'Have you had a head injury?'

'Oh yeah, I had an accident.'

'You look, actually, very good now.'

He agreed. He was made up, because it was the first time since the accident that his face had looked normal. The Botox smoothed out the lack of muscles and got rid of the indented area.

Botox is an injection. It comes in a powder which you mix up into a solution, a bit like making instant coffee, I suppose. Once it's made up, you inject it into the appropriate areas of the face. But the results are absolutely incredible, you can see the difference as soon as you've injected the face. All wrinkles just disappear.

People who have it, tell me it makes them feel so much better. It relaxes the muscles, it stops them being able to frown, and it also lifts up the face. Sometimes you get a bruise in the skin from the needle, sometimes you don't – you try not to get a bruise, but there's little vessels there, and inevitably sometimes it happens.

I haven't had too many things go wrong with the aesthetics work I've done, thank God. For me, the cosmetic procedures are incredible because they allow you to change somebody in a subtle way, so they look better, but you can't see they've had anything done. That's the aim of it I suppose.

And I sometimes get people come to me who are quite worried about having the first procedure, who say, 'I don't wanna look like that celebrity who looks like they're standing in a wind tunnel, or who looks like a melted Barbie doll.'

I take their hands. 'You're not going to look like so and so, you're going to look like you, but a bit better.'

It puts them at ease, especially when I explain I've had all the procedures I do, and more, so I know what it'll feel like.

I didn't start having anything done to myself until 2000, when I needed a bit of touching up, you know. A bit like how you have to maintain your house. That's how I think about it with my body, as the years are passing.

Mind you, some of my customers are in their twenties and obviously I wouldn't do it on anyone under eighteen. The procedures are classed as a prescription-only drug for people eighteen and over. Most of my customers are thirty to sixty years of age. I work with mainly women, but I also have quite a few men. It's across the board in terms of backgrounds and incomes, so I see all of life as we know it. It's not only rich people at all. It's really anyone. The procedures start at a few hundred pounds, and some people pay more than that for a designer handbag, so most people really can afford it.

And when people come and they say, 'Do I need to keep it up once I've started with it?'

I explain that well, no, you don't actually have to keep it up. If you decide that you like the result but for whatever reason, you're not going to be able to keep it up, it doesn't matter. All your skin isn't going to fall away, it just goes back to moving again. All my procedures, fillers, Botox, are non-surgical and so are non-permanent. It's a bit like having a haircut; eventually your body goes back to how it was before. I don't use anything that's permanent; the stuff I use dissolves after up to two years. And it's quite safe.

Although Botox is my most popular procedure, I also do fillers. They're probably the second most requested work.

A filler almost looks like glue, let's say. It's a gel, and you use a syringe to inject it. It plumps out lines, you can contour faces, you can give people cheeks, you can fill in hollows, you can augment the chin. It's quite versatile and is always used on the face.

Anything that I do to anybody, I'll always have it done to myself at least once or twice, because it's important for me to be able to say to people confidently, 'Well actually this might hurt a little bit, or this doesn't hurt' or yada, yada, yada.

You can use fillers in the upper cheeks. The nice one that I enjoy doing is filling in lips. I love doing lips. And I never make them look stupid, you know, giving someone the trout pout. I just have quite a knack with lips and make them look a little bit enhanced and it's really satisfying afterwards – for me and, of course, the client.

Occasionally you do get an issue with some people, but that's why with my nursing and cosmetics training you deal with those issues. You deal with the complications and you put it right for somebody. I would never walk away from a complication, and I always help someone out if anybody's got an issue.

I have some people come to me and they'll go, 'Oh I went to somebody for fillers and I'm sure she gave me water.' This woman explained she'd used a Groupon deal. The filler is meant to be a special liquid that dissolves over two years. Water would only last a few days and you'd be back to where you started; a complete waste of money.

'The fillers didn't work,' she said.

So I explained that you get what you pay for. If you pay next to nothing, then you'll get next to nothing. When it's your face you should be very careful who you're allowing to go near it. I know I am!

Of course, Lesley Ash and her lip enhancements always comes up when I'm discussing fillers with clients. I sometimes get people who say, 'I want massive lips, like a cartoon character.'

Because I've got morals and don't want people to leave me looking stupid, I say, 'Well, I'm not doing 'em. I'll enhance your lips – make you look like yourself, but better, with fuller lips. If you want comedy big lips you'll have to go somewhere else.'

I also do RioBlush which is carboxy therapy. It's carbon dioxide with a fine needle you use to inject under the skin. Used on the face, it rejuvenates the skin, and it reduces the appearance of stretch marks and scars all over the body. And you can inject it in the scalp to increase hair growth.

I had a woman who had a really large and visible scar. After this treatment, the scar has practically disappeared. I was so happy for her.

One of my friends, Alan, who's a doctor, does some work in Harley Street and I've helped him a few times. We've been on a few different programmes together, it's like Carry On bloody Doctor. We did a clinic with some hair transplant surgeons operating next door. When we went into the room, I said, 'Oh my God, it's filthy, filthy, dirty!' So I cleaned up our room because I'm a cleaning freak and I like everything nice and clean which you have to have for surgery and cosmetic procedures.

After a while, one of these hair transplant surgeons came in from next door. 'Oh, I have lost my phone. Did you see my phone?'

I looked up from scrubbing the sink. 'Phone, what'd you mean?'

'I can't find my phone, I left it in here.'

'Oh, I think it's in the bottom of the bin.'

After he'd rummaged all through the bin, he washed his hands. 'Couldn't find it in there.'

I smiled to myself. 'No actually, it wasn't in the bin, but I've cleaned up all your dirt and crap in here before we operate on our patient.'

Dirty bastards.

I also use a special facial cream – Endocare. It's a wonderful product which is made from snail slime. It's rejuvenating to the skin, you see. To make it, they have all these snails on this wheel which rotates underneath them as it extracts their slime. They sterilise the slime and then make it into this cream and serum. It's the Rolls Royce of facial cream, honestly.

I also use a dermaroller – you roll it against the skin, and the tiny needles make the face bleed, and then the skin rejuvenates after that. You can do it on hands, chest, face. I've seen some very good results with that. It sounds painful, but they're only small needles and it just pricks the skin very slightly.

CHAPTER FOURTEEN

Being a Botox Babe now

The reason I'm a Botox Babe, is because Botox is my most popular procedure – I sell loads of the bloody toxin. The reason for this, is because it's the most effective. You can see such a difference in someone's face right after injecting Botox into it. I've had it done many times, and my face is completely smooth and wrinkle free.

I don't do any actual cosmetic surgery because I'd have to be a trained surgeon to do that, which would mean many more years of training to be a doctor, then specialising in surgery. It's not for me.

I work with a cosmetic surgery clinic in Croatia, and refer my patients who are interested in cosmetic procedures. It's a great business relationship because the non-surgical procedures I do often go with the surgical procedures they can do.

The clinic approached me a while ago to ask if I'd be interested in referring patients to them. It was good timing, because at the time I wanted to have an eye lift. I said I wanted to meet them first, so they invited me over and did my eye lift for free. I paid for my flights but they did my surgery, and in return they recorded it. Afterwards I did a talk in Croatia about the procedure, how clean and quick the clinic was, and I'm very pleased to say that they've used it in their promotional videos.

One of my customers, who's also a friend, said, 'Oh, I'm going over to the clinic in Croatia, will you come with me?'

'Well, I can't really afford it at the moment.' I was having a bit of a lean patch, work-wise, you see.

'Don't worry about that, I'll pay for your flights and hotel.'

I love Croatia so I couldn't pass up an opportunity to go there again. 'I'll get my case!'

It was very interesting because I sat with her while she had it done, and we talked most of the way throughout. She had her eyes and face lifted. She looks twenty years younger now – but still natural, not like she's had work done, you know.

I think that's the trick with cosmetic surgery – if people can tell you've had it done, it's not been done right. You want them to make you look like you, but a good ten or twenty years younger, and on a good day.

I've had a mini face lift and an eye lift but I don't look like a melted Barbie doll, I just look normal really. Nobody's ever looked at me and said I look funny.

When I had the eye lift, I flew to Croatia on the Thursday, I had the surgery on the Friday, I flew back on the Wednesday and I was in London at a conference on the Friday, and all I had was one slight little bruise on the left eye. People's bodies are very resilient, and good surgeons try to minimise the bruising and damage, so you can heal as quickly as possible and get back to normal life, looking much better.

In Croatia it's about £1,200 for an eye lift. In the UK it's at least double that, so with flights and hotel, you're still quids in going to Croatia.

The biggest problem with the UK and surgery is there's too many bloody infections. The surgeons who work in private medicine also work in the NHS, and sadly the NHS is riddled with infections and bacteria like MRSA, CDIFF, and much more. Then the surgeons walk into the private hospitals with the same clothes on and take their infections with them. It's quite worrying.

When I trained as a nurse, the wards used to be clean. The cleaners used to report to the Matron and she kept them on their toes. Now, sadly, the cleaning companies often don't work for the hospital, so Matron can't tell them off. They're working for a different company, so Matron has to ring a call centre in Portsmouth or somewhere, and speak to someone who logs the call, then it gets escalated to the manager in the hospital, and maybe the manager will talk to the cleaners on the ward. Or maybe not. It's quite a shame really. Not every NHS hospital is dirty, but there are plenty that aren't very clean, in my experience.

In Croatia, it's absolutely pristine clean and there is no infection. The clinic I work with only does surgical procedures, they don't do any public health system operations, which would be their equivalent of the NHS.

As well as the eye lift, I had a mini face lift a few years ago. With a mini face lift they just take the skin off your face not your neck. A full face lift they take the skin from the neck as well, but my neck's pretty good so they didn't need to do that. They took about an inch, or two and a half centimetres off my face. They remove the skin, pull it tight, and then cut it off and then sew it back up.

When you get older, your face sort of goes downwards, and you have to be pulled upwards. It was a procedure I'd wanted for a while, and when the Croatian surgery offered it to me for free, as a thank you for the customers I'd referred to them, I couldn't believe it. I said, 'For free?'

'You'll have to pay for your flights, but the surgery will be free.'

'I'll be on the next bloody plane!' And so I was!

After the face lift, I went straight back to work the next day. I flew back and I had a bit of bruising and stitches, but nothing to stop me getting on with my life. It was amazing. I was so pleased with the result – it took a good ten years off me, I reckon. A good ten years of living and my face falling downwards was reversed with a few little snips and a tug to tighten things up! Marvellous.

I don't think I will have any more surgery because I'm quite happy with how I look now – younger, but natural, is the look I'm going for. I like to keep my body maintained regularly with facials, injections of Botox and filler and the odd nip and tuck now and again.

My clients for the cosmetic procedures come from all walks of life. About ten years ago, I had an appointment to do some Botox injections on a prostitute called Linda. When I first met her, I was chatting about her life and her holidays, and I asked her what she did as a job.

'I'm a prostitute,' she said, bold as brass.

'Fair enough. Where do you work?' I didn't know if she worked on the streets, in her car, house, or what have you. I didn't know how it all worked, so I thought as she's brought it up, might as well carry on talking to her while I'm injecting her face with Botox.

'I work in a brothel on the other side of Birmingham,' she said, then told me where it was, and asked if I knew the area.

Linda liked the Botox and at one point she was seeing me quite regularly, but sometimes she had a problem getting out of work for the appointments in my clinic. So I agreed to do the injections at her workplace – this brothel. I was pleased because I wanted to kill two birds with one stone: I was going to inject her and also give her an unwanted gift from a man I'd been seeing.

One evening, this man came round to see me. Stood at the door, he said, 'I've bought you a present.' He gave me a white bag with rope handles.

I thought, this might be something nice and posh from a boutique or a little gorgeous expensive gift. I lifted shoes out. Thigh high red black plastic stiletto boots with four inch heels and fake diamonds scattered over them like stars in the sky. If I'd ever worn them I'd have been over six foot tall. Not me at all. I dropped them back in the bag and said, 'That won't go in my vase!' Because I only like flowers. I let him in, but because I couldn't forgive him for the boots, I dumped him by email a few weeks later. So anyway, these boots were sitting in the corner of my bedroom and it seemed a shame to just thrown them away. I thought, Linda the prostitute might be interested in them.

A few weeks later, I went into this brothel in my lunchtime. Now what do you say when you're in a brothel? It's not like going to a hairdressers, is it? I stood next to the reception window where Linda was sitting. 'Are you busy?'

'No, it's Ramadam.'

'That's lucky. Shall we do your injections then?' I looked around the small square reception room with sofas along two of the walls and a pile of magazines on a coffee table. I couldn't do the injections there, because the door opened onto the dirty street. And the walls were bright purple and it was starting to give me a headache.

'Follow me.' She led me down the corridor into a room. She sat on the bed, I sat on the chair. I didn't want to sit on the bed because all I could think about was how many people had shagged on it.

So I did her Botox injections, and when I'd finished I said, 'I've got something for you.'

'Me?'

I took the shoes out of the bag. 'I think they're very you.'

She clapped and screamed and jumped up and down. She nearly had an orgasm on the spot, and before I could say anything they were on her feet. 'How much do you want?'

'Oh, twenty five quid.' Now I think about it, I realise I was very slow there. I should have asked for more, or should have asked for fifty pence every time she used them. Anyway, you live and learn. So, £325 better off and no hideous boots, I'm out of the brothel, and she's happily wearing the boots.

Anyway, I bumped into her in Birmingham about nine years later, and she said she was working as the receptionist in another brothel.

'Oh, Linda I'm so pleased,' I said. 'You don't do those dirty things anymore.'

She stood smiling at me.

'What happened to the boots?'

She looked side to side, because we were in Boots the chemist in Birmingham. 'I wear them on a Monday.'

'Why on a Monday?'

'When I see my clients. I wouldn't wear them at reception, it'd be a waste.'

So she's still doing the naughty things but only on a Monday, and she saves the boots for then! At least they're still well loved and she's getting good use out of them.

The fillers that I use for faces, I also use them for hands. You can put them into hands which makes them look so much younger. You inject it in and smooth it along, and it rejuvenates the hand. It tends to be older people who want this procedure because hands give a lot away with people; they can be very ageing. The fillers plump the hands up and make them look younger.

A woman in her sixties had this done and, when she left, she rested her hands on the table to pay me. She said, 'My hands look like my daughter's and she's in her thirties!'

'Bit of nail varnish and you'll feel like you're thirty again.' I smiled. It's so lovely when a customer leaves feeling better than when they came in.

I enjoy the cosmetic work because I can make a difference to somebody's appearance, which makes them feel better about themselves. I love Botox because it makes such dramatic difference to people's appearance. I'm a bit addicted to it, to be honest. I'm always having a bit of a top up with it. It's been proven that if you have the Botox injection, because you can't actually frown, it tells something in the back of the brain that you're happy, so you feel more positive about things.

Maybe that's my secret to keeping on laughing through all the shit life's thrown at me! Keep smiling, keep injecting the Botox, and keep taking the tablets! Three easy steps, the Mary Yates way to happiness!

Because of my nursing background and since I've had all my procedures done on myself, I'm always very realistic and honest to people about what they can expect and what's impossible.

Like I had one woman in her seventies show me a picture of a young woman. 'This is my daughter.'

'She's lovely, isn't she? You must be proud.'

'Can I look like her?'

I handed her the picture back. 'I don't fucking think so, love. You're about fifty years older. I can do a lot, love, but I can't do bleedin' magic!'

CHAPTER FIFTEEN

Mary's words of wisdom – Part One

Spirituality

From time to time I like to see clairvoyants. I don't go back to the same one, I like to mix it up a bit and go to different ones. I've been to loads over the years. I find them absolutely fascinating. I love how they talk about all aspects of my life: work, children, romance, money – everything, really. I think some people are sort of gifted in that way. Some of it comes true, some of it doesn't come true, or I should say, hasn't come true yet!

I saw one a while ago and she told me that I'm going to meet somebody in June, July or August 2016, and that my son's going to be a billionaire.

Well, I'm still waiting for the man to arrive and although my son's rich for someone his age, he's still not quite a billionaire. But I'm living in hope for them both to come true!

I'm quite a spiritual person as well, really. I do mindfulness and meditation sometimes if I'm trying to calm myself down, or I need to just focus on thinking about one thing – or not thinking about one thing, too. I go to the gym as well and I think that's very good for the old body – keeping it looking not so old. But I don't do yoga. I don't think I could sit in that position with me legs crossed.

Although I'm not religious, I'm spiritual and I believe there's definitely a life after death. There's so much research into it, that I don't think it is the end when you die. I think the spirit sort of leaves the body, but you're kind of still around. I believe there are ghosts and spirits, other worldly forces things like that. I'm very sure you shouldn't be frightened of them. Experience has taught me, the people you should be frightened of are the people in the living world, not the dead ones!

I believe you can feel the people you've known and loved, after they've died. I nearly killed myself by accident, driving alone. I went to see this man I'd been going out with, and I was so upset by what he'd said to me, it really affected me. On my drive home, I put my foot down, wanted to get a bit of speed up, get myself away from the bloke and how he'd spoken to me.

I thought the road was long, but it turned out that it was much shorter than I thought. Before I knew what was happening, the road had ended, and I drove through the traffic lights onto the main road. Fortunately, there were no other cars there, and somebody, something, turned the steering wheel and guided me across the traffic island, past a large tree. I ended up with just a little bit of a bump in the car where I'd hit the edge of the tree, but otherwise I'd have hit this tree doing seventy miles an hour.

Without a doubt that would have killed me.

I've been contacted by my dad after he died. I had reiki once – it's like healing hands, where they use their power to heal you but don't actually touch you. I was a bit cynical about it, but anyway – I was lying there, and this woman was doing this reiki to me.

She looked to the corner. 'There's a man sitting there with a dog.'

I looked at the corner and of course, no one was there. 'Where?'

'He's from the spirit world. I can see him,' she explained, still with her warming healing hands near my body.

'What's he doing?' I asked.

'He's watching and he's smiling, and he's stroking his dog.'

My dad had a great sense of humour, and he had a dog called Brandy, who would have been dead and with him again. He must've been watching me with this woman doing this so-called reiki, and if he'd have been alive, he'd have said something like, 'What the bloody hell you paying her to do that for? She's not even touching you! What sort of a massage do you call that?' But of course, all he could do then was smile at me, with that look in his eyes.

My Bad Habits

My only bad habit is smoking. It's a terrible habit. People say, 'Oh, you shouldn't smoke, it's bad for your skin!' Let me tell you, my skin's fine – although it has had a little cosmetic help along the way – but even so, I have the skin of a woman thirty years younger than me!

People also say, 'Oh, smoking's bad for you!' But here's the thing; smoking is something that I enjoy. I really enjoy everything about it – the ritual of lighting up, the smell of an unlit cigarette, the shiny plastic you rip off the packet, having a nice lighter, the talks you have with people stuck outside a bar or restaurant, having a ciggie together.

I love it all.

But I also go to great lengths so people don't know I smoke. I'll chew gum, spray perfume, nip outside quietly to have a crafty cigarette. A lot of people say to me, 'You don't smoke do you? You don't look like a smoker.' And I'm thinking, I bloody well do, whatever a smoker's meant to look like.

I can't stand to see people smoking in the street. I think it looks horrible, very common. So I tend to hide my smoking habit, but I do enjoy it even though it's terrible. It's a horrible habit, and one day I will give it up. One day.

What I Think About Drugs

I am totally against drugs and that's one of the things that really works me up. In Kuwait, they actually hanged a drug dealer, a rapist and a murderer. It was wonderful, it was on YouTube. I commented that we should send the man who set his house on fire and burned himself and his children over to Kuwait so he could be hanged. And all the do-gooders came out and said, 'Oh no, you can't.'

I am actually for capital punishment, an eye for an eye and all that. If somebody kills someone, then they should be killed themselves. After seeing this video, I thought the Kuwaitis have the right idea, they just hanged these people as justice for what they'd done.

Drugs get me so worked up because it's such a damaging thing for people's lives. It's not just the drugs themselves, what they do to your body and mind and how it takes over your life, but it's the drug dealers, what they do to their clients. It's also what people need to do to get the money to pay for the drugs – stealing, prostitution, all sorts.

Heroin is a terrible substance – it ruins people's minds, bodies and lives so quickly. I've seen how it takes people when I worked with the homeless, there were all sorts of substances there. While working with the homeless people, I helped resuscitate three of them from drug overdoses.

Money

I've spent a lot of money on cars – over the years, I've had loads of cars, loads of bloody cars. And my best car was my red Jeep which kept breaking down, which was fab. I kept being towed on it, but I loved it anyway – bright red and high up on the road, it used to make me feel like I was in some procession, with everyone looking at me. When it was working anyway!

I like to spend money on holidays. I'm going back to Croatia later this year, for my daughter's birthday, so that will be brilliant. I enjoy spending money on holidays, on having a good time.

Going through bankruptcy and coming out the other side, and even being ripped off for all that money by Dr Mohammed, were all such useful experiences – taught me so much about money.

I'm also quite emotional about money. I'm always looking at what I can afford and what I can't afford. The bankruptcy has made me more aware of that.

I used to have to spend money as soon as I had it, but now I'm a bit more careful. I don't like getting in debt now.

My parents looked after their money. My mum was the one who took care of the family's money. They both worked really hard at the factory, and they bought their own house, brought up me and my brother, never got into any debt, always saved up if they wanted anything. I don't know what they'd have made of me and all the debt and bankruptcy! Still, I've learned from that now. I won't make that mistake again. Or will I?

Spirituality

Sometimes I think it's sad that both my parents are dead – I'm an orphan now, but an adult orphan. Occasionally I just wish I could talk to Mum and Dad because I've done so much with my life. It's some comfort that I believe they can see me now. I'm not a religious person now, but I'm religious in my own way – I'm spiritual.

I like to believe Mum and Dad are still with me and hopefully they're quite proud of me and what I've achieved.

Being Myself

When I'm out there, meeting people, I don't put on an act – I am me, and I am me all the time. It's taken me a while to realise that if someone doesn't like me, that's their problem and not mine. It's much more honest to be yourself, rather than pretending to be someone else.

I like to smile and make people laugh in all my work and personal interactions, because that gets me through, and gets them through too. I try to have some banter and build rapport with people, whoever they are and wherever I meet them.

I read somewhere that everyone's fighting their own difficult battles in life, so when you meet people you should be kind to them – that's what I do, I always have a smile when I meet people.

Losing my Temper

Normally I'm quite easy to get on with and I don't very often lose my temper but if I do lose my temper you'd better watch out. I've had some bloody good rows if somebody upsets me, I can really give 'em a mouthful. I was driving down the high street in Droitwich once. A lorry had parked in a very inconsiderate place which was holding up the traffic. I wound down the window and said, 'Oi, mate, can you move over, you're causing a traffic jam?'

'Can't move.'

'Why not?' I asked.

'I'm doing a delivery and there's nowhere else to park.'

So I told him where he could have left the lorry, just round the back of the high street, but he wasn't interested. I said, 'If you're delivering something, why don't you get on and bleedin' well deliver it, and move on?'

I wasn't going to give up, because after he'd told me to mind my own fucking business, I got out the car and stood next to his door and told him to move before I called the police.

Eventually, with a chorus of beeping horns and applause from other drivers, he did move. He took great delight in sticking his finger up at me, and I just waved back, smiling.

I don't normally have arguments with friends, but I used to lose my temper quite a bit with Husband Number Two, the cruel violent one.

Finn said, 'I found this pubic hair in the house. What have you been doing?'

I think it was probably the babysitter's, it was absolutely nothing to do with me. I was expecting him to show me this pubic hair but he didn't, he kept shouting about it and whose was it, and what had I been doing with men coming in the house?

I knew he could be violent. He was shouting at me about the pubic hair, following me around the house, accusing me of this, that, and the other – everything was my fault apparently, right from World War II onwards, he seemed to reckon.

I stared him in the eyes. 'Look, I don't know anything about this public hair, it's probably the babysitter's, but it's got fuck all to do with me.'

But he wouldn't listen – he kept following me around the house as I was trying to make sure the kids were sleeping and get myself ready for bed.

I told him I didn't know anything about it and could we please change the subject? And he went right back round, the same old accusations and the same old arguments about this public hair. So I lost my temper with him and hit him as hard as I could and actually flattened him. H landed on the floor like a sack of potatoes and I carried on getting ready for bed and checking the kids were all right. He stopped talking about the pubic hair after that.

That was years ago. I can't remember the last time I lost my temper recently. I think as you get older you get more laid back, get better at just shrugging it off, so nowadays I don't usually lose my temper. If someone's annoying me now, I just smile at them, because that always winds them up a lot more.

My Creativity

I think I can be a creative person, but often I'm too lazy to do it! Doing the cosmetic injections, you've got to have a certain amount of creativity to do it well – to shape the face, and lips, and other parts of the body, to make it look natural and yet better than before. As for anything else, I just can't be bothered. I get other people to do everything else if I can.

I never clean my own car now; I pay someone to do it. I have a cleaner for the house, she's wonderful.

But doing the cosmetic procedures is definitely creative – I've got to use my eye to make sure the clients don't come out looking like Frankenstein or something, so that's an art in itself.

I can't sing, I used to really enjoy acting, as a child and teenager. Maybe I could've made more of it after school but I don't regret not doing that. I don't do regrets – pointless.

People From Different Backgrounds

I can embarrass myself anywhere! I don't really mind who I talk to, and I can talk to anybody and I can listen to anybody. I've travelled all over the world, worked with people of different backgrounds – Birmingham is a very culturally diverse city, more than London in some ways I think – and I've looked after all sorts of people. To me, people are just people. Black, white, yellow, orange, Jewish, Muslim, Christian, man, woman, working class, royalty, whatever, everyone has to sit when they shit.

I can and do talk to anybody and am good at making a rapport. I think if more people just saw others as people, not with all these labels, the world would be a much better place.

Biting My Tongue

I find it hard to bite my tongue. Actually, scrap that, I can't bite my tongue. If something's gotta be said, I will say it.

You know when you're sat at work and someone's saying a load of old shit and everyone else is sitting there nodding like bloody nodding donkeys and agreeing? Well, I'm the person who has to put her hand up and say, 'Why are we doing this?' or 'What's the point?' or my favourite 'This won't work because...' So much is down to common sense, and although nursing needs lots of common sense, I've learned there's a lot less common sense floating about than people think.

I am that voice of common sense. I used to work in a hospital at weekends and every Monday I would call the chief executive to complain about the lack of equipment or how there weren't enough staff working.

The chief executive would say, 'That's simply not true, Mary.'

'I was there. I saw it. There were no dressings all weekend.'

'I've spoken to the ward manager and there's plenty of dressings.'

'Then they're fucking well lying. I was there yesterday and there weren't any left. And don't even get me started on the staffing...' I would go on and on at him, because I can't bite my tongue if something needs saying, I will say it. I don't give a shit about what people think of me being a troublemaker, or a pain in the arse. I'm saying it because it needs saying and because no other bugger's going to say it. I will stick up for anybody. I will defend people to the hilt and I hate people being bullied as well. Bullies pick on people who can't defend themselves, and I am happy to swoop in and defend people who can't defend themselves. I suppose it's my nursing background coming out again.

CHAPTER SIXTEEN

Depression

We live in an extremely stressful world, and I think there's more people who suffer with mental illness than even just thirty years ago.

Mental health services are one part of the NHS – which generally I think is a wonderful organisation and a brilliant service for us to have in this country – that's under-funded. It drives me insane, it's one of my bugbears. There's a team near where I live in Birmingham, called the crisis team. One would assume, you call the crisis team, and it's there for people who are having a mental health crisis. But it doesn't matter what you say, or how bad your mental health is, they will never go out to anyone in a crisis in anything less than a month. It's absolutely shocking, this so-called crisis team, they're an absolute joke.

One of the reasons I'm so passionate about mental health is because throughout my life, I've had periods of mental health issues.

I've suffered from depression in the past, and I still cope with it on a day to day basis even now. I've not been well for periods of my life for as long as I can remember. It comes and goes – the crying and not being able to get up and other stuff like that. Then something will change for me!

Someone from my past was in the UK recently and he'd been bringing me down. He'd been threatening to kill himself and asking me for cash and I stupidly gave him the bloody money too!

I am definitely not going to entertain the idea of him coming back into my life. I am not going to talk to him and I have blocked him on Facebook. He makes me feel ill.

There are some people in life who are drains; who drain energy out of you. There are other people who are givers of energy. I've learned it's important to surround myself with givers of energy, with people who help me, and to cut out the drains from my life.

For my whole life, it's been a roller coaster of being in and out of depression. I am somebody who suffers from depression but I get through it every time. There's hope for everybody if I can cope with living with depression.

I had my first a nervous breakdown at nineteen years old. I was quite ill then. I've had about three nervous breakdowns, so I do empathise greatly with anybody with mental health issues. Because I've been there, got the T shirt and seen the Broadway show of it too!

The first one was definitely the worst. Having a breakdown was a terrifying experience, because I didn't know if I was ever going to get over it.

There wasn't one thing that made me have the breakdown, it was a lot of stuff, one thing after another.

It happened just before I got married and I suddenly went a bit peculiar. But the interesting thing is, even though I've been through these blips in my life, I still carry on working! I think for a lot of people, work is its own therapy. It gives you a reason to get up and have meaning in life.

I was in such a dark place at that time that I actually took an overdose. I can't remember now if they pumped my stomach, because it was a long time ago. I took a load of paracetamol but anyway, I was fine in the end.

I was admitted to hospital for about a week, and my mum and dad were quite distressed about it, which you would be, but then that treatment sort of sprang me out of it, and I was fine again.

I was staying on a psychiatric ward. I can't remember much about it, but I remember I had this treatment and they were going to give me loads of it, but I only had three cycles in the end. But afterwards, oh my god, when I returned to the ward, the headache was terrible. I could hardly see straight and I felt sick, but it did the trick – it lifted the darkness.

The treatment itself was electro convulsive therapy, or ECT. They put an electric current through the old brain, you see. I remember laying down on the bed, and they strapped me in so I didn't struggle. They put this thing in my mouth to bite on, so I didn't bite my tongue off, then they attached two electric pads either side of my brain, a bit like headphones, but above my ears. Then they turned on the electricity.

But I'll be honest with you now, and I'm not ashamed of this, I take antidepressants even now, to this day, and I'm absolutely fine with it. I'm better on them, because if I'm not taking them, I'm not good. Without the tablets, I find myself falling back into a depression pretty quickly.

If I had to describe what depression feels like to me, I'd say it was a dark hole going deeper and deeper, and you just can't seem to get out of it.

A while ago, I was going to see this Buddhist guy, who was fantastic, and he was teaching me all this relaxation thing, and meditation and mindfulness, and one thing and another. Anyway, he told me it wasn't good for me to be on antidepressants long-term, so he persuaded me to stop taking them, and got me onto this natural non-prescription herbal medication.

And then, all of a sudden, I just couldn't stop crying. I was waking up in tears, I was crying all day, I was going to bed in bleedin' tears – everything just made me cry.

This went on for a few weeks and I thought, I can't carry on like this, I'm not coping. I thought, if I'm not careful I'll end up back in hospital with the metal pads strapped to my head again, and I didn't want that!

I phoned my doctor and said, 'I can't stop crying.'

'Come down and see me today,' he said.

I arrived at the doctor's surgery and told him what this Buddhist man had said, and how he'd tried to help, and in the middle of it, while I was telling the doctor, there they were again – the tears kept flowing out of me, rolling down my cheeks, my mascara and foundation was all over the place. I didn't even know what I was crying about, but it just all seemed so terrible, so black and dark, the tears came springing out of me.

My doctor held my hand. 'If you're still crying on the Tuesday, you're gonna hang yourself by the end of the week, so just start taking the tablets. There's no shame in it.'

'Yeah, give me the tablets for God's sake.'

The Buddhist man had done his best to help me and show me you can take various herbal things to help with moods, but unfortunately it just didn't work for me. I need the prescription drugs. It's just how my brain works – or doesn't!

When I came out of hospital years ago, after the ECT, I felt much better – like I was human again, like I was part of the world, and like I could go on with my life again. It's a real weird thing, depression, that dark place it takes you to in your head is terrible.

What a bloody sad thing, Robin Williams killing himself. He was such a jovial guy. What annoyed me and showed me that so many people don't understand depression, was when they said, 'Oh, what did he have to be depressed about?'

What most people don't understand is that depression doesn't have to actually be about anything, you can just get it. And that's exactly how it's been for me.

Lots of people have a problem being on their own; spending time alone, but although I'm a very sociable person – I love spending time with friends and meeting new people – me, on my own, I'm fine. I can talk to myself, and I can even answer myself, but is that worrying, maybe? Taking holidays on my own are always very funny, but I'll tell you more about that later. I talk to anybody, and anybody talks to me. I've got one of those faces that screams, 'Let's tell her a story and make her cry!' I'm fearless; it's the only way to be, to live your life I think.

I've had a lot of knocks over the years but I don't let anybody or anything get the better of me.

As well as the mental health, I've had a lot of people who've done terrible things to me, dragged me to hell and back both mentally and physically, but I live through it. I carry on. I have to and that's where the humour comes in as well. I love to laugh, I love to make people laugh. I've always managed to pick myself up and carry on. I've got this strong core of drive and self resilience. I always come back fighting, and I will always have the last word.

So if you're struggling with mental health issues, remember – there's no shame in taking the tablets. And talk about it too. I hope that by discussing it here, in this book, it will show others how common depression is, and how it doesn't have to be about anything. You can just get it. A chemical imbalance in the old head!

CHAPTER SEVENTEEN
Holidays and relaxation

I enjoy holidays and I like to relax then. I'll have a massage or a sauna when I'm on holiday, that really calms me down, lets me unwind. To be honest, I don't think I ever really relax except when I'm on holiday!

I find it quite difficult to read when I'm in the house - there's always something else going through my mind, thinking about the business, ordering stock for a procedure, booking a consultation with a client, or organising my next nursing shift, There's always something going on. But I do enjoy a good book on holiday. My favourites are by Patricia Cornwell, she's the one who does the murder mystery stories. I enjoy romantic stories. And if I want to do a book in about an hour, I'll skip through a Mills and Boon. 'cos you always know what's gonna happen in the end, and they're quite short. But I don't like reading anything too complicated. I wouldn't sit and read something like Shakespeare, or anything literary or hard work, that's not my cup of tea at all. I like a good story. And I like a book that can make me laugh.

Wilt on High—I tell you what, I can remember sitting on holiday by the pool, sipping my drink, sunbathing, and absolutely belly laughing through that book. The other people at the hotel were giving me funny looks, thinking, what's she on, that woman, but I didn't care. I just carried on laughing, right through to the end of the book. Bloody brilliant it was.

Somebody actually bought me a bloody Kindle and I can't stand it. I know others swear by their Kindles and Nooks, and whatever else there is, but not me. There's something about the Kindle and it's a bit of a demon, I'd rather have a book. Every time

I pick it up, with its screen, little buttons and plastic casing, I think I'd rather have a book. I've tried to use it a few times and I can't – it's like they've made it too complicated with the buttons and the links to shopping online, and all that. It's like reading on a bleedin' computer. I see it laying on the table, I think, oh, I can't be doing with this. In fact, I should actually sell it I think! Anyone fancy a hardly used Kindle, let me know! I like a good old fashioned paperback book.

When I'm at home, I like to relax by going to the gym, and swimming. Circuit training, I do like laughing at that, especially at other people! You know people who take it really seriously? That cracks me up, when they're staring straight ahead and not talking and not even breathing, it seems, between exercises. I feel a lot better after going to the gym. I like going with a friend; it's nice to go with somebody because she looks a bit more stupid than I do sometimes, and other times I look more stupid than her. We take it in turns looking stupid and laughing at the people who take it all too seriously. I've just read that back: and except for reading on holiday, even when I'm relaxing, I keep going at a hundred miles an hour! But that's just who I am, it's me.

I also relax by going out for drinks or a meal with friends, and having a laugh with others, but that goes in phases – sometimes I'm always out, other times I stay at home and don't see anybody.

When I'm on my own, I like to lay in bed and watch the TV. But generally I find it difficult to relax and do nothing, unless I'm on holiday.

I went to Naples with a gay friend. Once we'd settled into our hotel he said, 'Oh, I'd really like to meet somebody over here.'

'Oh, let's get you a profile on Gaydar.'

A few hours later, he said, 'I've got him, I've got him! He's messaged me, likes the look of my profile and wants to meet.'

'Told you it'd work!'

'He's coming down tonight to meet in our hotel. I thought that was safer than meeting him at his place.'

'Good thinking, Batman!'

Later that night, my friend was sitting in the hotel bar.

I made sure he was settled, had a drink, didn't feel nervous. I pointed out the window. 'Look, I'm gonna go to that bar over the road, so bring this bloke to the bar where I am for something to eat. I'll be nearby. And then go back to our room and you do what you wanna do. Don't go anywhere near my bed or my shoes, and I'll amuse myself in the bar.'

So anyway, I'm sitting in the bar and getting a bit plastered, like you do, enjoying myself, chatting to the locals, watching the world going by.

When it was all over, at about two o'clock in the morning, this gay friend called me to say he'd finished.

I crossed the road, back to the hotel, and even though it was so early in the morning, Naples was like the bloody Wacky Races – cars weaving about everywhere. I got propositioned five times between the bar and the hotel.

Back in our room, I asked him, 'So what happened with this bloke?'

'Oh, he was married.'

'How'd you know?'

'Well, he said to me - you can do to me what my wife can't.'

'Bloody hell, what did you do to him?'

'I came in his mouth.'

Fair enough, I thought. and shrugged. 'Did he swallow?'

'No, he didn't, as it goes.'

'How rude!' Well, that was enough for us for the night, so we both went to sleep.

The next day, we were drinking in the bar over the road from the hotel, and I said to my friend, 'Did I tell you what happened to me last night?'

'No. It can't have been better than what happened to me.' He was quite competitive, you see.

'I had a shag in here.'

'What do you mean – in here?'

'You know when you were eating, here, in that corner? I was there.'

'That's disgusting. I thought you were keeping an eye out for me, making sure I was OK.'

'I was. I also had a shag, too. Is that all right with you?'

So I told my friend how the barman, he couldn't have been more than about twenty five, he sort of plied me with vodka. Well, he didn't need vodka really. I find it easy to pull people – it's my animal magnetism and I've got a good sense of humour – we'd been having a good laugh in the bar together. He was dark haired, nicely built, possibly did a bit of weightlifting. And he must have sensed the timing was right, because one minute we were chatting and having a laugh and the next he was pulling the shutters down and I remember thinking, thank God I've had some vodka. Then, of course, all my clothes fell off, and I ended up over the table in the bar, with him giving me one. To this day I can't remember much about his face or what colour eyes he had, but I can still picture his big cock like it was yesterday! Like I said, I am a trollop, but I love it!

I went to Dubai with my friend, Penny, who I treated as a present, because she was having a bad time in her life. We decided to go on one of these Jeep safaris. We were dressed for it, both in trousers so we could ride a camel in the desert at the end of the safari. I'd borrowed Penny's wrap trousers because I didn't have any trousers of my own. I dunno if you've ever been on a safari, but you get in a Jeep and you go up and down, and up and down the sand dunes, and a lot of people are sick with the motion. Well I wasn't sick, fortunately – I've got the constitution of an ox.

I spotted a guy. I thought, he looks quite handsome, a bit Basil Brush, he had a moustache and wore their traditional clothes, it's a bit like a dress, but for men.

Our driver, he was nice enough, but he didn't have any teeth, said to Penny, 'Do you wanna come and drive my car?'

Basil Brush said to me, 'Do you wanna come and drive my car?'

'Oh, OK.' So I climbed into his Jeep and he drove into the desert for a while.

He stopped the car, then showed me a video on his phone of a woman being shagged by a horse.

I pushed it away. 'For God's sake, turn that off, it's disgusting.'

We drove a bit more and then we arrived at a collection of tents pitched in the desert. I got out of the Jeep and looked around for Penny but she was nowhere to be seen.

So this Basil Brush bloke, he suddenly started to kiss me.

I thought, oh, I'm not really that comfortable with this, but I did kiss him because I fancied him, it just seemed a bit sudden. He hadn't even introduced himself, just lunged in with the bristly moustache kiss. I didn't let him touch me, he didn't see under my clothes or anything, all he got was just a little kiss.

But the next minute he pushed me down on the sand, then he put his cock between my legs.

I was really glad I had Penny's trousers on, and not just a dress.

Then, as he was kissing me, he shuddered a bit and I felt a wetness between my knees.

He said, 'Oh, sorry, I've messed up your trousers.'

'Don't worry, they're not mine.' I thought, oh my god, here we go again, why's it always me?

He kept apologising and helped me clean up the trousers as best he could.

Eventually Penny turned up, with a really red face, holding her hands in the air, waving to get my attention.

'What have you been doing?' I asked.

'You will not believe what happened, we got stuck in the desert, our phones didn't work, we had to dig the Jeep out and somebody came to help, and they got stuck as well.'

'You're back safe now. I need to tell you about your trousers later.'

Later that evening, when I told her what had happened she laughed. 'Only you, Mary.'

When I was married to my Turkish husband, I had my gallstones out, and I decided to go on holiday on my own, a nice bit of relaxing me-time. Or so I thought.

I went to Majorca. I was exhausted from work and stresses with the Turkish husband, and as soon as the plane was in the air, I fell asleep. I know some people get all stressed about flying, worrying about it crashing. If it crashes, it crashes, I don't give a shit.

When I arrived at the hotel, feeling very relaxed, I said to the guy on the desk, 'Where's your badge?' I'm a bit of a badge person. I like to know who I'm talking to, so when I complain, I can quote their names. I've always done jobs where I have to wear a name badge, so why shouldn't other people?

I tapped my nails on the reception desk. 'How many kids are staying at this hotel?' The hotel felt odd with no kids running around and screaming. I wanted to relax but I wanted a bit of life on the holiday.

'None.' He pinned his badge to his uniform.

'Really, why?'

'It's an adult only hotel.'

Pensioners only hotel, more like! And everybody there had lost somebody. I tell you what, I nearly hanged myself. I had five people crying on me. It was really sad. I've got one of those faces that people think, I'll tell her. 'How are you?' I asked this man.

'Well, my son's just died.' He started crying.

And I was thinking, oh my god, I'm going to need a holiday from this holiday when I get home.

It was all inclusive so I was stuck in the hotel really.

Later that year I went on my own to Ibiza for a week. Arrived at the hotel, hadn't had anything to drink or eat, and all I wanted to do was sit down and chill out. The receptionist gave me my key and made some gesture of where I had to go for my room.

Well, I walked and walked and walked, and I was thinking, I'm gonna fricking well die here from dehydration. I couldn't find my room, so I walked all the way back to reception. 'Where's my room? I can't find it.'

So the receptionist, no apology, no offer of a drink, nothing, she called a man over who walked me to my room.

I actually thought I was going to die, it was about a twenty minute walk away. I think we may have left the hotel and ended up in a different hotel. By that point I could hardly see straight. I tripped down a step, banged my knee, twisted my ankle, twisted my arm. When I eventually got into my room, I rang reception. 'I don't want this room! It's too far from the pool and bar and everything. In fact, I don't even think this room is in your hotel!'

'I can assure you, Madam, it is one of our best rooms.'

'I want to be moved!'

They moved me to a room back in the main hotel building, by the pool. I settled into my room, unpacked, had a glass of water, lay on the bed for a bit, then realised I was so hungry, I went into this restaurant. I thought, there's some very strange people in here.

I ate my food but there seemed to be lots of adults making strange noises and banging on the tables. I thought maybe they're excited to be on holiday, and ate my food alone in silence.

I thought I'd explore the hotel a bit so I went downstairs into the entertainment room which had an animation show on.

There was a man who had Down's syndrome wearing a red wig and a yellow dress, holding two balloons, and miming I am What I am.

And at that point I thought I'd suffered a head injury when I fell earlier. I looked around the room which was full of mentally and physically disabled Germans on their holiday. I lie not.

Because I'd come on my own, and I was sick of my own company by this point, I took a seat to see what the rest of the entertainment for the evening would be.

There was a girl with Down's syndrome wearing a nappy and every now and then she screamed and banged her head on the table.

It was a fucking mad house – and I've worked with homeless people and in hospitals but this topped anything I'd seen before.

These people were treated like VIPs in the hotel as it was their holiday. I thought I'd better make the best of the situation so just got on with it, having my holiday around the disabled people as they had theirs.

One day I left the hotel to visit the beach and as I sat there in the silence, surrounded by normal people, I found I missed the lunatics, so I had to go back to the hotel. The whole two weeks I stayed there, I never saw any of the disabled people fall over and I fell over twice and I was stone cold sober!

I went on my own to relax and read a few books by the pool, and it felt like I was back in my nursing days looking after people again.

I don't very often get particularly frightened, but there was one incident where Kate and I were in Egypt. We had to sit on the sand and watch belly dancers and eat the Egyptian food, then we went on a camel to go to the star gazing farther into the dessert. The camel ride caused Kate a lot of stress because she decided, when it was too late, that she didn't like camels. Her camel kept being bitten by another camel.

'Just kick it,' I said.

'Mum, I don't wanna be here.'

We got off the camels and saw a few stars, which was a bit underwhelming, to be honest. We stared at the stars for a while, that was it.

Then all of a sudden, they shut everything down and it was pitch black.

As we were walking, in complete darkness, suddenly from nowhere a load of feral cats jumped out at us. We carried on walking, even though we couldn't see a bloody thing, then some lights came on and these guys came to collect us, to take us to the hotel. I didn't show I was scared because I knew Kate would then really worry. I carried on calmly hoping we'd be OK, and when the lights came on again, I knew we would.

I wish I hadn't bothered with the bleedin' star gazing now. It was nothing to write home about and scared us both shitless afterwards.

CHAPTER EIGHTEEN

Internet dating – physicality and sex

I like physical contact. I like to kiss and hug my friends. Sometimes, when I've first met someone, I will give them a hug and kiss on both cheeks. Some people don't know how to take that, but it's me; it's what I have to do. I like to touch and to be touched, in a sexual and non-sexual way. I enjoy sexuality, I think that's really important.

In a relationship, sex is important and not just in one, too – I'm often found in an Ann Summers shop stocking up on goodies!

I'm not embarrassed to talk about sex. I don't see why anyone should be. I don't get all this, no sex please, we're British! It's natural, it's normal, and if it's between two (or more) consenting adults, what's to be ashamed about?

As for me, I just enjoy sex. You could say I'm a bit of a trollop, if you knew how many men I've had. But I'm not ashamed of that either. It comes back to me being a very physical person. I like everything about sex: the anticipation, the games people play as they work out if they are going to have sex, the spontaneity of it happening, and the feeling of sex itself.

It's funny too isn't it - sex? If you're not having a laugh when you're having sex, I think you're bloody well doing something wrong! The noises, and the mess and the fun and the sex – it's all hilarious, I think.

A friend once asked me if it's worse to have no sex than to have bad sex. I thought long and hard (ha ha) about it, and can honestly say, I don't think I've ever had bad sex. For me, all sex is good sex, because it's happening, because I'm experiencing it, I'm having it, in the moment. It's a bit like an animal, isn't it? I am Mary, hear me roar!

Anyway, I say all that to explain why I got into online dating. In 2006 I really got into the whole internet dating thing. Every time, I felt like I had met the one, or at least the next one, and so I'd jump on a plane and fly to Italy, Spain, France, wherever these blokes lived, and I'd have a wonderful time. And the next week, I'd be back on the websites looking for the next one.

I'm a trollop. There, I've said it. I am a trollop.

Judge me if you want, but I couldn't give a shit.

I've never been hurtful to anybody, but you know I am very physical and I do like sex, and I like the pursuit of sex too. The chase. Like they sing in that musical, I'm just a girl who can't say no.

When it comes to men, love, sex, I think I'm very clever but I'm also very stupid.

I meet somebody and I think whoa, this is good. And it's good for a while, and then when it's not so good, it's onto the next one. I'm quite a passionate person.

I told you that I like people, but especially, I like men. I have some female friends, but I prefer the company of men.

And I don't like anybody trying to chat me up when I'm out, because I think in a way I'm a little bit of a control freak. I have to sort of control things, so I'm the one doing the chatting up. With a fling, I like to be in charge of saying this is what's happening.

As I discovered, there are a lot of scams with online dating. People pretend to be anyone and I'm just the biggest sucker. And I fall for the scams every bleedin' time!

In the middle of this mad internet dating period in my life, while on holiday with my kids, I received this email and a picture of this guy who I thought actually looked pretty dishy. He had sort of salt and pepper hair and looked pretty well-preserved, in his thirties. We emailed back and forth, and agreed for him to come round to mine in a few weeks, when I was back from holiday.

One evening, he rang the doorbell and I opened the door to this bloke with pure white hair. Not a speck of grey or black, no bloody salt and pepper, this was like a load of cotton wool on his head. I was a bit shocked, didn't know what to say. It was definitely the man I'd been emailing because I recognised his face – which in fairness, was pretty well preserved but with maybe a few more wrinkles and lines.

'Hello, you'd better come in,' I said. I'm a bit stupid really, I should have smelt a rat, but he was there, on my door, I wanted a shag, and he was offering one, so in he came – in more ways than just through my door!

Well, we had a few drinkies, and a few nibbles, and then dinner – I rang for an Indian takeaway to be delivered – and we chatted about things we'd emailed between us, my holiday, his journey, and how he'd never been to Birmingham before, and thought it was farther away than it had been. I don't remember much of what we talked about because, as usual, all my clothes fell off.

We were in my bedroom, in bed obviously, and off he goes, having sex with me. I don't remember the conversation but I can remember his body was covered in dark hair, and he had a big cock, and he knew how to use it.

I think he made me come twice that night so, despite the white hair, his equipment was all in good working order. He went home at the end of the evening and that was the end of that.

A few weeks later, I was driving down the motorway and my phone rang. I answered it and this female voice said, in a very thick Italian accent, 'Is-a that-a Mary?'

'Yep.' I wracked my brains for who I knew with an Italian accent, but came up with nothing, so I thought I'll just leave it to run its course and see where the call takes us.

'You... you... you met my Raymond.'

Well, the while haired bloke with the hairy body and the big cock had told me his name was Mike anyway, and I didn't have any clue about this bloody Raymond she was on about. I assumed Raymond was a cosmetics client of mine. 'Really?'

'Yes.'

'What did he have, Botox or filler?'

'No, No, you had...a fag.'

'Yes, I smoke. I might have had one of his when he was here having the treatment.'

'No! Shag, shag, shag!' she was screaming down the phone at this point.

So I told her to fuck off and put the phone down. Anyway, that was that, but for a few days she kept ringing my mobile and left a message: 'You, you are-a big, you are-a fat, you are-a ugly, you wear-a the red-a shoes, and you have a dirty kitchen.'

Well, the only thing that really upset me was the dirty kitchen, because you know, I was spending forty quid a week on a cleaner to keep the kitchen clean at that point, and it was bloody well spotless. The rest of it didn't bother me really.

I eventually spoke to this woman, and it turned out that this Raymond was an absolute shit. I managed to convince her to throw him out, which she did.

He wasn't married but he was seeing this woman, he'd gone back to her after seeing me and given her my phone number, which is why she called me. He must have told her I'd slept with him – that I'd lured him in or something!

The girlfriend – we got on quite well in the end, I ended up counselling her on the phone for a while – she was Italian, loaded, had a couple of Zara boutiques in London, and she had a million pound house and a big BMW or Bentley, or some big expensive car. She kept saying how Raymond was terrible, and she didn't know what to do about it.

I said, 'Do you know what? The best thing you can do is kick him out. He's a piece of shit, kick him out.'

'Well he's done this, he's been off here, he's been unfaithful with this woman, and another woman...'

'Look, he's a piece of shit. Get rid of him.'

She started asking me all sorts of questions. 'Well, what did you do, did this happen? Did you do this together?'

I thought, I'm putting a stop to this, right away. 'Look, I'm not prepared to discuss what we did or didn't do in bed together. What you need to understand is he's unfaithful and you've told me he's done it loads of times before, so you just need to get rid of him.'

I thought there was no point in having a post mortem of what he did and didn't do in bed with me; we slept together, he'd been unfaithful. End of.

And she actually did get rid of him, she told me. I was pleased for her in the end.

And then a few months later he just happened to ring me and said, 'Oh, hello.'

'Is that Raymond stroke Mike?' I asked.

'I want to see you again; I want to make love to you again.'

I'd had enough of the whole thing by this point – the counselling of the girlfriend, him pretending to be someone he wasn't, so I said, 'Do you know what mate, fuck off and get your pension.' I put the phone down.

This was quite a few years ago. I was really into the internet dating big time and I met loads of guys. Thinking back on it now, I realise I was a bit crazy 'cos I used to go to Italy to meet them. I'd go away for a weekend and, like, meet somebody and think oh God, they're fucking nice and just get on a plane meet them, and then come back to do it all again the next weekend with another man!

The Italy thing: I flew out there and I met one guy who was dynamite – great fun personality and great in bed too – and then I went out to Naples three times, where I met three different men.

I think I've got a thing for Italian men – must have, all that romance, and music and wooing me into bed – not that it takes much to get me into bed!

I went to Pisa as well and met another man but that wasn't so good, not at all. Over the internet, we'd been winking at each other and flirting and sending sexy messages between Pisa and Birmingham – sounds like a romance novel doesn't it?

But when I actually got there, it turned out he wasn't particularly very nice. We did sort of have a bit of passion – and when I say passion, I mean I shagged him – but other than that, he was not so good.

During this time, I would go onto MSN messenger and then I'd talk to, you know, different men I liked the sound of. And then I saw them either on web cam or we exchanged numbers and we'd talk on the phone for a bit. I preferred the web cam because you can see what you're getting then. Then, if I was still interested, I'd have a date with them. And I got through so many different men. Unbelievable, I am such a trollop really. My excuse is I'm a very physical person – I enjoy sex, I love men, I like passion, basically.

That's my excuse and I'm sticking to it!

I mean, luckily I've never caught anything, 'cos I've always been careful and obviously I didn't get pregnant, and although I put myself in some very dodgy situations, taken so many risks, I'm still alive to tell the tale.

I had a couple of years of internet dating after I'd divorced from my second husband. I wanted a total change, you see. I wanted to have some fun, and this internet dating gave me access to all these men all over the world, and so much sex. I used to jet off, meet up with a man, shag all weekend, jet back home to work on the Monday. Then I'd be back again somewhere else, shagging another man the next weekend.

I think I was always looking for someone better, someone new, someone different. I suppose being married for fifteen years made me realise how much else there is out there for me to experience, and experience it I bloody well did! It was fun.

My parents would have been horrified. They'd have thought I was such a trollop, but do you know what, I wasn't doing anyone any harm, and I was having some fun I'd missed out on, the whole time I'd been married to Flynn. The kids were old enough to look after themselves, and so it was time for some me-time.

In a relationship, I like to be in charge – I like to be the one in the driving seat deciding what we do, where, and when. But equally, what I really want, is a man to look after me. A man to sweep me off my feet, like in those Mills and Boon novels – a millionaire or a rich sheik to sweep me off my feet and take care of me. But the thing is, I'm not sure how those two things work together – me being in charge and having a man look after me. Perhaps that's why I've been married three times!

All this time when I was internet dating, you see, I was still on the lookout for my ideal man.

I've never looked for money in a man. But now I think about it, I would like to meet somebody who would actually like to look after me and be good for me, instead of me attracting these unsuitable men.

I'm quite an affectionate person and I think that's quite important. I'm not frightened to actually put my arms round somebody and give 'em a hug – even if I've only just met them.

Sometimes that scares people, but what is there to be scared of from a hug from me? It's just kindness.

I met this guy on Plentyoffish.com – and I thought he was having a heart attack. He told me he was as fit as a fiddle, he'd never had any this, that, and the other, said I didn't have anything to worry about sleeping with him.

When he arrived at my place he injected himself with insulin.

'I thought you were fit as a fiddle,' I said.

'Oh yeah, I forgot to mention that. Diabetes.'

We went out for this date, an Indian restaurant for a curry, which was the best bit of the evening, to be honest. I didn't even like him, he was rude, arrogant, full of himself, not interested in what I had to say at all, didn't listen, and the worst thing was, he had no fucking sense of humour.

I got this taxi to bring us back and he got a bit amorous, leaning towards me, trying to kiss me. I pushed him off and said, 'You've no chance, mate.'

Somehow we ended up in my bedroom and he was lying on the floor, next to the window, clutching his heart. 'I've got this pain.'

'Is it going down your left arm?' I asked, thinking it was a heart attack, because that's what one feels like–I know from my nurse training. I rushed out, got my stethoscope and thermometer and checked his blood pressure and temperature. It all seemed normal, but he was still going on about how much pain he was in.

I thought, oh shit, here we go, because he wasn't exactly in the first flushes of youth, if you know what I mean. I ran downstairs to get him some sodium bicarbonate and water. I ran back to my bedroom.

He lay on the bed, clutching his stomach, and then the bastard projectile vomited up my best bedroom curtains. It was absolutely fucking horrendous green, pink and white sick everywhere. It was like the Little Britain sketch where the woman throws up like it's coming out of a hosepipe. I thought he was dying.

Nothing happened between us. I wouldn't let him, and he couldn't have done anything if he'd wanted to, because he spent the whole night in the toilet vomiting. I came out in a rash as well.

I think it was the prawns, I don't think they were fresh.

I was doing a clinic in Birmingham and I told Colin and Steve - this gay couple of nurses I worked with – what had happened. Colin offered to help me hang the curtains up after they'd been washed, because I knew I'd fall off a ladder, and break my neck if I did it on my own.

So a few weeks later, I was hanging them up again with Colin and I said, 'Do you know what, the bastard never paid for those curtains.'

'At least you got a good shag out of it, Mary,' Colin said.

'That's the sad thing.' I put the curtains down to rest my arms for a minute. 'I never did. I didn't fancy him. He was fucking terrible.'

'Not even just for a shag?' He shook his head.

'Not even just for a shag. I wouldn't let him go near yours, never mind mine, darling!'

And, do you know, actually the cleaning didn't work very well and those bloody curtains shrunk as well. I had to throw them away in the end, and I never saw the puking bloke again.

This one time, I was in the middle of shagging another guy who had an asthma attack. He clutched his chest and tried to breath but couldn't. He pointed to his mouth and his eyes stuck out as he gasped for air. I rifled through his bag and gave him his inhaler, but it didn't seem to do much. So I rang for an ambulance and had to send him off to the hospital to get sorted out. It was shagging me, you see, when he had the attack. I'm just fucking dangerous. I'm like one of those insects who eats the male insects when she gets a shag. Mary the black widow, I am!

I met this man called Tim, but I didn't sleep with him straight away – it didn't feel right somehow.

He rang me from his hotel and he said, 'Will you join me?'

'No,' I said. Instead, I sent him a bunch of flowers to his hotel in Bristol.

Even now, he still talks about these bloody flowers I sent him.

At the time, he rang me when they arrived and said, 'Nobody's ever done that for me before.'

Eventually I did meet him, and he was hilarious because he sent me this message saying: I need to see you and I must see you, I am aching to see you.

All this over the top stuff.

I was a bit wary of him, because some woman had told me he was a bad person and she sent this message to all of his email contacts, saying everyone should watch themselves around him, how he'd stolen money from her and he'd hurt her, all sorts of lies.

He had to lay low for a bit while all this blew over – because it was just a pack of lies. So during this time, he came to see me and we flew out to Spain together where we had a ball – drinking, dancing, partying, and shagging, it was fabulous. He came back and had to face the music for all this rubbish the woman had accused him of, and then unfortunately he had to resign from his job in the RAF.

He's still a great friend, we have a good laugh together now, nothing sexual any more. He moved onto another woman and I moved onto another man – these things happen, but he came into my life for a reason and we're still great friends. I think that's wonderful.

He's one of my best friends now. If I'd not met him and shagged him, I wouldn't have him as a friend, so it all worked itself out in the end, I suppose. It works as a friendship but not as a relationship. I suppose it's because I snore! Maybe we could have been together, but I dumped him because I'd buggered off to Scotland to see this fireman I'd met online. Me and Tim had been together for three months at that point.

I didn't want to end it with him, but I had this offer of a weekend in Scotland with a Scottish fireman and I said to Tim, 'Do you know what, I'm going off to Scotland.' And I did!

The guy I went to see was a part time fireman and full time postman. He turned out to be in a relationship with somebody else who actually contacted me, to tell me he wasn't single and what did I think I was doing seeing her boyfriend and one thing and another.

Oh, it just goes on and on and on. With me anyway!

My friend Tim, he likes to stay with me, and we like to have a laugh together. We made up this social media profile called The Lady Likes To Say Yes, and he pretends to be me and insults people on Lycos and MSN and Plentyoffish. You can swear on Lycos now, they've changed it recently. It's great fun and, fuck me, Tim's been swearing loads, pretending to be me. We have a wonderful time together; much better than if we were a couple, I'm sure.

I met this man online, he was a solicitor, so I thought I'm onto a winner here, this one's going to be well educated, very proper, well spoken, all that jazz. I was at his house, and bearing in mind I am very anti-drugs, he said out of nowhere, 'Do you want some coke?'

'Coca Cola?' I asked, like a naive idiot that I am, because when someone says Coke that's what I think of.

'Coke coke.' He pulled out this square pyramid of white powder in a little plastic bag, then poured a bit onto the mirror that was resting on the table. He got a five pound note, rolled it up and, with a credit card, made it into a few lines of white powder. Then he stuck the note up his nose and sniffed it up, like a tiny little Hoover. He looked up after he'd finished and said, 'Do you want some?' Like he was offering me some sugar in my tea.

I don't know why, but I had a little bit. 'I don't want you looking at me. Look away.' I stuck the note up my nose and sniffed along the line of white powder, just like he'd done. Some of it blew off the mirror when I blew out with my other nostril.

To be honest, I didn't really know what I was doing, but I just got on and did it. It fucking burned my nose, I can tell you. Fuck knows why anyone would want to do that for pleasure.

A while later we were chatting and having a laugh, and he looked up from between my legs and said, 'It's worked then?'

'What do you mean?' Because I didn't feel any different really, just the same, no rabbits jumping out of the wallpaper, or flashing lights, or funny feelings when he touched my hands, none of that shit I'd read about you're meant to get when you do drugs. This was just like, us sitting there, chatting, nothing really.

'You're talking a lot!' he said.

Now, I talk a lot all the time anyway, so I don't know what he was on about. Besides, he was trying to have this conversation with me while he was kneeling between my legs and giving me oral sex.

'Don't talk with your mouth full,' I told him.

And he got right back to it, stopped talking, and got back down between my legs.

He was good at it, to be honest, because plenty of men aren't much cop at the old oral sex, in my experience. Which was lucky, because he couldn't get it up, so that was all I was getting from him that night.

Going on all these internet dates is hilarious but also it can be terrible, because you never know who you're going to end up with. But it's constant. Meet one, don't get on, meet another, do get on, have a shag, meet another one.

I met a guy online a few months ago, and he said, 'Meet me in Kidderminster.'

I know, it's hardly Paris or Venice, but it was about half way between where we both lived. I met him in a café in Kidderminster where we had two cups of coffee, had a chat about ourselves, our journeys, what we did with our lives.

We paid and stood outside and he said, 'What do you wanna do?'

'I dunno, what do you wanna do?' Expecting him to say, let's go for a proper drink, or a meal, or something.

'Really, I'd like to take you back to mine and shag you.' Bold as brass, like it was nothing, I mean, and all he'd done was pay for my coffee.

'Do you know what mate, you've got a fucking chest infection, you've no chance.' I just walked away, thinking cheeky fucking bastard, didn't even offer to buy me dinner or a drink!

I've slept with loads of men I've met on internet dates – and I love it, the thrill of the chase, the chat, the banter, and then, obviously, the sex.

Have I ever met a man just for sex? You know, like this dogging where people meet up in car parks and shag each other's wives and husbands, or these websites where men shag married women in their cars. I've done loads of things, but I've never done that, I know it's not for me.

I suppose, when I go on these dates, there's always a little bit of me hoping, wishing, wondering if it'll be my next husband, or boyfriend, the romantic man who'll look after me. I think, going in just for sex, meeting someone only for sex, feels a bit different, a bit like an animal would do. I know plenty of people do it – gay men, straight men, straight women, and probably lesbians too – and hats off to 'em, whatever makes you happy as long as it's not hurting anybody, but I know it's not for me. I think it's because, in my heart of hearts, I've got a romantic hopeful core to myself. All the shags and all the men, I'm hoping it will end in romance, like in one of those Mills and Boon novels I love reading.

CHAPTER NINETEEN

Husband Number Three

I met my third husband, Tad, online. I'd been doing loads and loads of internet dating in about 2007, back in its heyday. I saw him online and I thought, oh my God, I really like him. I thought, I've got my house, I've got my car, I've got my cosmetics business, it was almost like I was buying a designer husband.

What you need to understand, is that among all the online dating blokes who'd been hit by the ugly stick, or who had been divorced four times, or who had a face like a smashed crab, Tad was young, and very easy on the eye. It was almost like I'd got everything in a way, I bought him too. And literally, in less than two weeks, I flew out to Istanbul and met him. And then I flew out four more times between September and January, and then he came to live here in January 2008. I sort of fell head over heels in love with him. We got married in 2009.

I definitely bought him though: I bought him over to England. I paid for all his education while he was here. I paid for the wedding. I paid for everything really.

I don't remember his proposal – funny that, since I'm all about marriage, maybe the marriage is more important than the proposal. Anyway, what I do remember is how the wedding was a right fiasco. We couldn't get married here in the UK, so we got married in Turkey, where he lived. While I was out there, my dad died, so I came back early and it was a bit surreal really.

But sadly, Tad was a gambler, a real bad one. I don't know whether I shut my mind off to it, but in the end you know, it got too much. So we got divorced. But he was only young, he was about twenty odd years younger than me, something like that.

The whole time I was married to Tad, I think I sort of ignored the fact he was a gambler. I knew it, but I ignored it. He was without doubt, the most stressful person in the world, ever.

He would ring me in the middle of the day and shout down the phone, 'Mary, Mary, oh, you've gotta come home...'

And I'd dash home, and I'd ask what's the matter, and he'd say, 'Oh, I've cut my finger.'

I'd be like, 'And? I was at work, I've gotta get back.'

'I've lost this money,' he would say, like it had disappeared into thin air.

Yeah, in the gambling machine, I'd think.

'I've hit my car and I had to give a woman some money because I hit into her car,' he said.

'I've ruined my clothes so I had to buy some new ones,' was another one he said.

Once he told me someone had stolen his shoes while he was at work, so he had to fork out for a new pair.

I think in my heart I knew he lied to me, but I didn't want to believe it; I wanted to believe he was the perfect designer husband I'd bought, to add to my perfect life.

Oh, how wrong could I be?

He'd bet on anything – horses, greyhounds, who's gonna win X Factor, anything. He told me proudly how he'd won £25,000 in Turkey some years ago on the horses on an accumulator, and how he blew the lot in five days. He took eight blokes over to Dubai – expensive hotels, gambling, entry to night clubs, eating at the most expensive restaurants. You think it, and he'd spend his money on it. All gone in five days.

When Dad first saw Tad, he looked him up and down, then said, 'Bloody hell, he's only about twenty five!'

'Well there's nothing wrong with your bleedin' eyesight is there?' I said.

Dad had guessed his age spot on.

I think Tad was sort of looking for a mother type figure, in a way. I mean, at first he absolutely loved me, he was kind and loving and caring, it was everything I'd hoped for. But unfortunately he just couldn't stop gambling. I couldn't keep track of how much of my money he gambled, but it's probably about

£60,000. Could have bought myself a nice little house in Birmingham with that! I was only married to him for three years, and that's how much he ripped me off for.

Give him his due, once he was in the UK, he always worked. He was a waiter. He was very good at what he did.

The kids were OK with having him as a step-dad – even though he was about their age. At first they were just happy for me, because he made me happy, he loved me, we had a great time together. But in the end, the kids understood why I had to end it. The gambling was out of control. I didn't want to go bankrupt for a second time! Once was traumatic enough!

CHAPTER TWENTY

Going bankrupt

Since I was a little girl, I've always wanted to strive and stretch myself to live a more interesting life than my parents did. Don't get me wrong, there's nothing wrong with working in a factory your whole life. Mum and Dad were both happy. But I knew from being a teenager that I wanted to be a nurse, and do something bigger and better with myself.

The nursing led to the aesthetics, the Botox and all that, and that led to me working with Doctor Mohammed. And working with him led to me going bankrupt because I'd borrowed all this money as part of the business we had together.

It just all suddenly came tumbling down around me. One day I thought, hang on a minute, what do I do about all this debt?

I saw this solicitor, Miss Ellie, and she said, 'The best thing is for you to go bankrupt.'

She helped me go bankrupt and also keep my house. I don't know how I kept the house, to be honest.

Miss Ellie said, 'As long as you keep paying the mortgage. you'll be OK.'

And she was right, thank God!

Once I'd started the process, there was so much I had to do for the bankruptcy. It's not just a five minute job, as I found out! I was up and down the motorway trying to sort things out. Oh, I've got to go to court. Oh, I've got to pay Miss Ellie £2,500 to process my bankruptcy for me. There was a lot of paperwork to fill in. Forms and more forms all over the place.

I had to go to this court in Gloucester, and they grilled me about why I'd gone bankrupt. I can't remember what they asked me, because I said I had to keep my phone on because my father was ill, and he may go at any moment. I was in a bit of a daze at the time, to be honest.

However, at one point, I was going to actually walk away from it all – the house, the mortgage, the lot. I thought I was going to lose everything because of the debt. But then I thought, hang on a minute, I can't walk away, this is my house! I realised that, at the end of the day, I actually really like that house. And even though it's still an interest only mortgage, the mortgage is quite doable now.

So, throughout the bankruptcy, I kept paying the mortgage, and I kept the house, and it's where I live now. I had no personal loans or anything against the business. The car was repossessed because I couldn't keep up the payments. They didn't take anything from the house, though, so that was something I suppose.

In the middle of this. I found out that Dr Mohammed, who I'd gone into business with and who'd got me into all this debt, had gone to see my solicitor, Miss Ellie as well, so she ended up dealing with both bankruptcies.

Me and Dr Mohammed both went bankrupt at approximately the same time. Him for £876,000 and me for £165,000.

Later, I found out that Miss Ellie had collaborated with the doctor and they had a business together. Corrupt. Bizarre. Unbelievable. It was just the weirdest thing. It's like one of those daytime TV programmes you see. You watch it and you can't believe that stuff like that really happens.

Well, trust me, it happened. To me!

The stress was unbelievable. I had a breakdown. There's no two ways about it. A proper breakdown. It was pretty bad. I was completely gaga. I can't remember it really.

I went bankrupt on 12th November 2008, and the lead up to it was about two months. Miss Ellie led me through the process, step by step – that was what I was paying her for really.

I got the paperwork together and the solicitor submitted it for me. I had to go to court two or three times to explain my case, and I had to pay at the court too, every time. So it actually costs quite a bit of money to go bankrupt. And it's not an easy process either.

That two month period of going bankrupt was one of the most stressful periods of my life. It was a confusing time, because I'd made the decision to go ahead with it, and then I had to get the paperwork together and find the pieces of paper, fill in the forms, and what have you. When I saw it in black and white, the amount that I owed, I thought, how could I have done that? £165,000. I remember staring at the figure on the form and blinking, hoping that it would go away. But it bloody well didn't! I couldn't believe I'd got myself into this situation.

Through this whole period, there was one saving grace. I never owed a person the money. It was a bank who I owed. They'd given me a loan a credit card, not an actual person. The debt was wiped out and it was never anyone's personal debt.

With Dr Mohammed, a lot of his debt was personal, and over £100,000 was what he owed me.

I'm not sure how it would have changed things if my debt had been to actual individuals. I don't owe anybody personally a penny. That's really important to me, even now. I remember holding onto that during the whole process. Because when you go bankrupt, they just write off the debt, so if it had been to actual people they wouldn't have got the money. But the banks, they can manage without it easier than an individual. That's what I reckon anyway.

The Turkish husband was actually quite good at this point. He looked after me. Fair play to him. My husband was making sure I was eating and drinking, and taking my tablets, because I was struggling with the simple things at the time.

I had a couple of nurses coming to the house. A psychiatric nurse and a psychiatrist coming to see me, because I was just so screwed up by the whole thing. I was in a fog. I was literally just managing to get from one day to the next.

While I was going bankrupt, I also lost my job. I think I went a bit doo-lally too. That must have sent me over the edge, I think.

Dr Mohammed shut up his surgery and got rid of me. I was gone from my job straight away. Over that weekend, when he said he was shutting down the business, he took everybody else back on, but not me.

While I was unwell and going through bankruptcy I was still

having to work because I had to pay my mortgage. I realised that, without the job at Dr Mohammed's surgery, I had to start working in a different way. I got a job in a health centre and did some practice nursing.

I still managed to keep my aesthetics business. And I'm very proud of that.

Dr Mohammed then reported me to the Nursing and Midwifery Council (NMC) to try and get me struck off. That was my livelihood. If I'd have been struck off, I wouldn't have been able to practice as a nurse, or do any of my aesthetics work either. I wouldn't have had any way of supporting myself. All those years of nursing, he'd have wiped out, just like that.

Luckily, the NMC didn't find anything wrong, so I kept my registration and carried on working as a nurse. I don't know what I'd have done otherwise. I see being a nurse as a part of who I am as a person. I've wanted to be a nurse from a young age and it's something I know I'm good at, so having that taken away from me would have really hit me hard.

Luckily it didn't come to that.

I, however, have a file about two inches thick on this doctor, and all the illegal, immoral, terrible things he's been up to. But nobody would listen to me. The police, the Crown Prosecution Service, the General Medical Council, they all said there wasn't enough evidence. So he got away with it.

Anyway, after the whole process, eventually I bounced back. And I'm still here to tell the tale.

I now think going bankrupt was the right decision for me, looking back. But with my friends I always advise them to look at alternative options. Because of the stress involved. Going bankrupt really isn't an easy or a cheap option.

A very good friend of mine is forever grateful for me not allowing her to go bankrupt. Instead she's gone into liquidation.

In the middle of going bankrupt, I went to my son's school about my money problems, because I knew I'd have problems paying the tuition fees. It was his last year at the school before going to university, so I knew it was important for his education and he couldn't be moved to somewhere else.

I sat in the headmaster's office and tried to tell him about the bankruptcy, and losing my job, and my car being repossessed, everything. I remember trying to count the things off on my fingers, and trying to show him bits of paper I had in my handbag. I was so mentally ill I could hardly put a sentence together.

The headmaster just said, 'I can see you're really clearly mentally ill. We're going to let your son attend the school free for his final year.'

I thought, well, you're right, I am loop the bleedin' loop, because when I talked, it came out as gibberish.

The headmaster said, 'Don't worry, your son is such a clever lad, we're happy for him to be here for free.'

And then, when we went to get my son's exam results, I shook the headmaster's hand and thanked him.

He said, 'Don't worry, you've got a good son there.'

Now it's all over – having gone through six years with the bankruptcy hanging over my head, not being able to borrow money, to get loans, having a mark on my credit rating – I can borrow again. But I have to be very careful. I've reflected a lot about it, and I'm not like I used to be – reckless with money. I'm much more careful now.

CHAPTER TWENTY ONE

Divorcing Number Three

Not long after going bankrupt, I went through the second worst period of my life of recent times. My third divorce.

With this husband, I got to the point where I couldn't stand it any longer. The gambling, the lying, the drinking. This was supposedly a good Muslim man who drank like a fish, smoked like a trooper and was very disrespectful.

For instance, in my home, where we lived together, he used to smoke in the bedroom, put his feet on the table, and do all sorts of disrespectful things that really, really pissed me off. It pisses me off even now, when I think about it.

He had no humour and I find that very hard to deal with in other people. As you know, laughter is so important to me. Somebody without a sense of humour is like a blank page to me.

He'd get very angry too. He had a terrible temper on him.

Sometimes I'd just sit on the floor with my head in my hands, because I'd had enough of the arguments and fighting and shouting.

He'd say, 'Get up, get up. You must get up off the ground!'

I'd look at him. 'No, I'm not getting up. I've lived with one violent man, I'm not going to live with another. If you want to shout at me, shout at me, I'm not getting up off the floor. You wanna talk to me, shout at me, shout at me from where I'm sitting now.'

And again, he'd tell me to get up, tell me to look at him, tell me what to do.

He was nothing like my second husband who was violent too, but this one, he did hurt me once, and I got the police in.

One evening, he rang the police and said, 'My wife, she is hitting me.' And all the time he was hitting himself in the face. He grabbed my arm so hard that he left marks on it.

Big black marks up my arm that ached when I moved. I remember thinking, here we go again, another man who's gonna hit seven shades of shit out of me.

Eventually the police came in response to his call.

I was shaking with anger and in pain.

He looked at the policeman and then pointed at me. 'She's hit me.'

And I was just looking at the two policemen. I held up my arm and there was all these black hand marks from where he'd hit me.

He stared at the policemen. 'Let me take my clothes off, she's covered me in bruises.'

One policeman said, 'There's no need for that. Whose house is it?'

'It's my house,' I said.

My husband shook his head in disbelief. 'I always have to go, she can go this time.'

The policeman said, 'No, no, no, you've got to go, sir.'

By this point, my husband was hitting himself in the face. He totally lost it. They escorted him out of the house.

He used to tell me about the money he'd made from gambling.

'You should sell your soul to the devil, because that's the only way you're going to get money for gambling.'

He just used to walk away without even looking at me.

I was sad that the marriage was ending, but on the other hand it was a relief to get rid of him. I couldn't keep up with the stress. Every week there was a disaster.

'I've crashed the car, I've gone on the ice,' he would say.

You're probably wondering, how come I married him? Well, he wasn't like that when I first met him. He sort of accumulated. His little habits and ways got worse and worse, little by little, until he was a totally different man from the one I'd married.

The worst over all was the gambling. I think I turned a blind eye to it initially, thinking it was a little hobby of his, like fishing or gardening I suppose. I didn't know how much he was spending on gambling until it was too late. Way too late.

One day, I'd been to work and I'd done a long nursing shift and I'd got a sandwich for £1 to save some money, because I had gone through the bankruptcy at this point and was trying to watch the pennies. Anyway, when I got home, I went through his wallet and saw the receipts.

I know I shouldn't have gone through his wallet, but we were basically living on my money at this point and I wanted to know what he was spending some of it on. He had spent £367 during one month in pubs. And one receipt was a really good meal for sixty eight quid and I'd been walking around buying a sandwich for £1 to economise.

I was so angry. I wrote him a letter, my hands were shaking as I wrote it: Do you respect me? How can you do this to me?

I handed him the letter and asked him to read it.

He got out of bed, looked at the piece of paper, then ripped it up.

'What have you done that for?' I asked.

'I don't need to discuss it.' He left the room without even looking back at me.

We never discussed it again. I knew how angry he'd get if I tried to talk about it with him, another time.

Fair dues to him, he was a great talker. I think that, along with how easy on the eye he was, was one of the things I found attractive about him when I first met him. He liked to talk. He liked to chat about himself.

Unfortunately, when I'd got married to him, I realised that, as far as he was concerned, it was his right, to him, to do exactly what he wanted. Regardless of me. Forget me.

He took an overdose once. The two ambulance women from hell arrived. He'd taken a lot of tablets.

I rang my GP for advice because the ambulance women were talking to him like they were psychologists instead of taking him to hospital.

The GP said to me, 'Tell the paramedics to take him to hospital. He's taken an overdose and that's what he needs, not to sit down and tell them how it makes him feel.'

I relayed this to the paramedics and eventually after a lot of to-ing and fro-ing, they agreed to do as the GP had suggested.

I found out from my husband that, on the journey in the ambulance to the hospital, one of the paramedics was slagging me off. How unprofessional!

I arrived at the hospital and, understandably, I wasn't in a good mood. I'd had enough at this point, between the husband taking the tablets, having to fight for him to be taken to hospital, and then the paramedic slagging me off and disrespecting me during the journey.

I saw this ambulance woman at A&E reception and even though I'm not very tall, I'd got some heels on. I walked over to her, and pulled myself up as tall as I could. 'Oi! Show me your name. You are going to so regret the day you met me.'

'What do you mean?' She stared at me, mouth open and eyes wide, like she was completely innocent, silly cow.

'Wait and see, love.' I reported her to the ambulance trust. I had two ambulance officers out to do an investigation on her. I found out later that she got suspended from her job. It might sound a bit harsh, but her behaviour was absolutely appalling – both to my husband, by not giving him the care he needed, and to me by slagging me off to her colleague and my husband.

That night we were at the hospital for hours. Waiting and waiting. Bearing in mind my husband's taken an overdose, I couldn't believe how long we had to wait. Eventually he saw a psychiatric nurse. It was an absolute joke.

This nurse didn't even want to speak to me. She'd assessed my husband, checked his mental and physical health and reckoned he was OK.

'What are you going to do then?' I asked, arms folded across my chest. By this point, I was well and truly cheesed off about the whole bleedin' thing.

'What do you expect us to do?' She looked up from her clipboard and chart.

'Section him. He's unsafe,' I said.

'What makes you say that? How are you qualified to diagnose that?'

'He's stolen drugs. And he's taken an overdose to try to kill himself.'

'We don't know that yet.'

'I'll tell you what, I've got a good idea, shall I lock all my drugs away at home?' He'd tried to kill himself and had stolen the drugs, and they said he was OK, I couldn't believe what I was hearing.

After that, when it all got too bad for us to live together, after the overdose and the violence, he went to stay at one of his friends' places.

When I realised my third marriage was ending, I remember thinking, isn't this terrible? Not really, I was actually thinking, next! That's not true either. I was really and truly thinking, I've got to get him away from me.

I've no regrets about divorcing him. It only took about six months. It was actually quite a simple divorce. The easiest of the three I've had, really.

The solicitor was brilliant.

Right near the end of the process, I nearly changed my mind about going for the decree absolute. I said to the solicitor, 'I think we'll hold back on this. Maybe I don't want to divorce him.'

The solicitor looked me in the eye across his big wooden desk. 'Oh no, you won't.'

For some reason, I was warming to the husband again. After how he'd treated me during the bankruptcy, and because the divorce took a while to come through, I sort of took him back under my wing.

The solicitor said, 'Look, if you want to get married to him again the next year, you can, but this divorce is going through.'

Of course, I never wanted to marry him again the following year. I was relieved I was shot of him.

It was pretty simple really. No kids involved. To divorce him, I never had to pay him any money. Why would I have done, since he took me for about £60,000 of his gambling debts? He never walked away with anything, except what he'd had out of me through his addiction to having a flutter.

The children weren't around at the time. In fact, when I told Joseph about getting divorced from Tad, he said, 'Well, I know he likes to drink, and he likes to gamble.'

'It's a bit more than that.'

The divorce cost about £1,500 and that was it, it was sorted. It felt like a positive end to another crappy shitty period of my life.

It left me wondering whether I was ever going to be able to find a man as passionate as me, to love me. But just because it would be difficult to find one, I didn't let that stop me from looking!

CHAPTER TWENTY TWO

Mary's words of wisdom – Part Two

Having A House Built For Me

I've had two houses built for me – where I live now, and the one before, and all I can say I've learned is, I wouldn't bloody well do it again. No fucking way! I could write a book on being ripped off! Everybody involved ripped me off – the builders, the plumbers, the electrician, the decorators.

I did stupid things, like paying a lot of people in cash, I won't do that again. I learned how important it is to make sure you have what you want in writing, none of this 'oh yeah, we'll sort it out when we get there', business.

If a builder can cut a corner and do something in an easier way, he will, even if that's not how you want it to be built. I had to be there every day, on their backs, checking how things were coming along.

While I was having the house built, I rented another one for a bit – to keep me out of the way of the builders and all the mess. Also, it's a bonus having a working toilet and somewhere to cook food. It took a long time from the builders putting in the foundations until it was actually a liveable house: they put the roof on pretty quick, but then it's all the internal walls, and the electric points, and water, and heating. I couldn't have lived in it, not until it was almost done, so renting somewhere was sensible – the one sensible thing I did, I suppose.

I have had solar panels put on the roof of the house. Because it's all electric – oven, central heating, everything – it is simpler that way, I thought. So apparently the electric grid pays you if you sell electricity back to them, or something like that! I don't really understand it, but when the builders explained it, I was convinced it was the best thing to do. And so I did it of course!

It's worth it, now it's all finished, but the day I moved in, the builder never put anything in the rooms we'd agreed— electric points upside down, holes left in the walls and floors, rooms not decorated. It was terrible. On top of moving house, I had all this, so it was very stressful.

And then, the cherry on the top of the dog shit was, I lost one of the cats. I thought he'd never come back, 'cos he'd done a runner from the house I was renting, but a friend helped me get him back. We were running all over the garden and streets, calling his name, rattling his cat food box and banging the tin of Whiskas. Then one day, bold as brass, he turned up, meowing and wanting food and a stroke. But that's cats for you, isn't it?

Loving My Neighbours

I sold the house next door to the new one to a lovely couple, who I call Mr and Mrs Bucket because they're so posh. I put some CCTV up outside my house to protect the car and house, because there had been a few burglaries in the area.

One day, not long after the neighbours had moved in, and when I was still in the middle of sorting out a list of problems with my house as long as my arm, Mr Bucket came round to mine and said, 'You've got a camera.'

'And?' I said, with a shrug, wishing he'd leave me alone and get off my doorstep so I could get back to my next bollocking phone call with the builder.

'It's looking at me.' He pointed at the camera on the edge of my house. His face was pretty red like a beetroot at this point.

So I slowly closed the front door, then checked on the camera and where it was facing. It was facing my car, nowhere near Mr Bucket's face. I opened the door and with a smile, said, 'Mr Bucket, I hate looking at your face, so why would I want to watch it on my camera?'

'You seem a bit upset.' He frowned.

'You know what? You have no idea, goodbye.' I wanted to say

he'd got the good deal with the house I'd sold him because it was perfect, while I was stuck with my half-finished, upside down house and weekly shouting matches with the builders, but you know, sometimes I don't have the energy for another row. So I just closed the door, rang the builders, and gave them a right good bollocking.

Pets

I like pets very much, I think they're good to have around children, and even if I'm in the house on my own, I never feel alone, because I've got a pet for company. Now I've got the two pets: Mo and Tiger, and they're like guard cats. They sit at the front guarding the house. Cats are so easy to look after, and fortunately my neighbours are very good, they always feed the cats if I'm away.

I've always had a dog since I've had my own house, but not at the moment. The last dog I had, it broke my heart, but I had to find him another home in the end. He was a Doberman, he was huge, he looked like Scooby Doo. But he was so bloody clever, e could open the door with the key. He would turn the key, push the handle down and, as he went out, he'd bark, 'I'm out again.' He'd be off up the road, annoying people. He was beautiful, but in the end I thought, I can't do this any longer. I couldn't handle the stress of him getting out and being run over, or running up to a small child and doing God knows what.

Although it was sad to let him go, it was the right thing to do — he's with a wonderful family and he's got a really good home.

When the children were young, we used to have Monty the Weinerama. He used to love fishing and, because we're not far from the river, he used to go fishing quite often. If we caught a fish, he used to run up and down the bank, so excited they'd caught a fish. He used to love it, barking away as if to say, 'Oh, they've caught a fish!'

That was quite a few years ago, and maybe one day I'll have a dog but not at the moment, because I'm always out and about with work and it's much more to look after a dog than cats. I'm glad the children grew up with dogs, because they are such wonderful family pets and it means they've got the memories of playing with them. Cats, you can't play with in the same way – well, you could give it a go, but I don't think they'd be too happy to fetch a stick!

My greatest weaknesses

I've thought about this long and hard and, really, I don't have any. That probably sounds quite arrogant. I'm not saying I'm perfect, but I don't see things wrong with me as weaknesses. I write everything down so I remember everything, I'm a real writer-down-of. I can look back on things that have happened years ago, and it's all written down. Although I'm not really a perfectionist, I do like to strive to get things right. I'm very organised – I suppose I have to be, with my home life, my family and my three or four jobs.

Having said that, although I don't have any weaknesses, I can sometimes be too emotional about things. I have talked about this with the woman I see for counselling sessions.

Because I can be too emotional, some people take advantage of me, and I need to sort of back away from those people. I've got to work out the best way to do the backing away. I'm a generous and giving person, and then some people take the piss out of that.

Some friends and colleagues phone me to ask questions and make use of my knowledge of nursing and cosmetic work. I can be on the phone for hours because I try to help them, and they come back and ask more questions and more questions, so I've got to pull back a bit.

I am definitely a people person. I will help anyone, and especially want to help my friends and colleagues and family. But it becomes too much when it's all a one way street – always them asking me for favours, or for advice, and I'm not getting anything back from them.

It's my fault, because I allow them to take advantage, and afterwards I think shit I've gone and done it again, why have I done that? It's part of being an outgoing, generous person and it can be quite draining, which is why I've got to look at how to pull back from some people. There, I do have a weakness – being too generous and giving, that's a weakness! I knew I wasn't perfect.

Winning The Lottery

I don't know what I'd bloody well do. It's quite interesting because I don't very often do the lottery, and I don't really think about what I'd do if I won it – that doesn't occur to me. I don't win anything on the lottery very often, so that's probably why I don't think about it much.

I know what I wouldn't do if I won the lottery — I wouldn't give it all to fucking charity, that's for sure! I can't understand these people who win the lottery and then give it all away – it's your money, spend it on yourself or your family – charities have got enough people giving them money.

I'd spend it on my family – they're the most important people to me, much more important than charities or anyone else. If I won the lottery, I wouldn't have to carry on working. Mind you, I know I'd go bleedin' well round the twist if I stopped working – I've been a workaholic since I was sixteen, so I'm not going to stop now. I'd still carry on with the nursing and cosmetics work because I really enjoy working.

My personal mission statement

It's quite simple – same as most mums I expect: to be happy and to look after my kids and make them happy.

I always strive to do my best in everything I do, and I think I manage that, but overall for me it's mainly my kids. I want them to be happy and secure. Being a mum is one of the best things I've done in my life.

When people look back at your life how do you want to be remembered?

I'd like to be remembered as somebody who laughed a lot. When I'm dead and buried, many years from now, hopefully, I want people to think of me, or stand by my grave and chuckle to themselves and think, Mary, she was a bloody good laugh, and she made people chuckle.

Money

I've grown up with not much money, worked and had periods of time when I've had enough money, and then had times when I've had so much money I didn't know what to do with it, and then I've lost it all. So I've had a variety of different experiences with money.

The most important aspect is that money gives us choices, and for that I like it. I like the feel of actually holding money, notes, coins, it reminds me of the work I've done to earn it, and how it's giving me choices. When I spend cash, I feel I'm really spending the money. I'm not so keen on credit and debit cards or cheques, because it doesn't feel real to me and I don't really associate that I'm spending the money. I've also had credit card fraud against me, which isn't possible with cash. Even the credit card fraud, although stressful at the time, didn't somehow feel real, because I hadn't seen the money being spent. Maybe that's why I got into so much debt working with Dr Mohammed in the cosmetic surgery business – all the loans didn't feel real, because I never saw the actual notes and coins. Now I've thought about it, I think that was why!

I like spending money, because I like to have nice things in life – cars, clothes, holidays, food – who doesn't?

Being Taken Advantage Of

Some people in my life really irritate me and I need to obliterate them. There are some people who draw on me, and it gets to the point where they're using me, and that's not a good feeling really. So I need to sort that out and try and work out how I'm going to get rid of them. I've not really done that before, because I'm so generous and giving and some people take advantage of it. I don't really know how this will go for me – it's a whole new world of friendships and awkward conversations, but I like new challenges and I know it's something I need to deal with. My counsellor will, I'm sure, help steer me through this, but at the end of the day, I'm going to have to work it out for myself.

I have obliterated some people from my life who are all take, take, take, but there are always new ones. New, negative people I need to deal with. And every time, it's not like I enjoy it. I don't rub my hands together and think, I'd love to obliterate these people from my life. It's difficult. I don't enjoy it. But as I've got older I've realised that, if a friendship isn't working and you've tried, it's best to just get rid and move on.

A Kindred Spirit

I've known many friends and colleagues throughout my life but, without doubt, my special friend Annie is my kindred spirit. She is a kind, generous and helpful person, and somebody I feel very comfortable to be around. The only way I can describe it, is that she sort of guides me. I've known her since about 2006.

It's quite interesting because she did a clairvoyance reading for me, and she told me somebody was going to really stab me in the back, which turned out to be Dr Mohammed, not long afterwards.

Even now, sometimes Annie does clairvoyance readings for me, but it can be a bit difficult because she knows me really well. The whole point of a clairvoyant is that they don't know you, so they are genuinely seeing into the future of your life, without knowing any of your background. Even so, I still value Annie's guidance and friendship very much, even if she can't do the clairvoyance readings for me.

Mobile Phones

So much has changed since I was a kid, but the biggest thing is, bloody hell, how we've all got mobile phones. I actually wish, in a way, we could blow up all mobile phones because they're a fucking nuisance. They have taken over everybody's lives, their friendships and family, and I wish they didn't exist. The problem with mobile phones is, they seem to ring all the time, no matter where you are, what you're doing, and who you're with; they're just really annoying. We all use them, I do, you do, but sometimes I feel they're actually more of a bind, really – more trouble than they're worth. The biggest problem is, they're a distraction sometimes from what you're meant to be doing.

When I see my children, it really pisses me off how they're sitting there and they're more interested in what's happening on their phones than with me, that really irritates me. If you're with someone, you should be with someone, not physically sat there, but mentally somewhere else.

Being Impulsive

I do everything I want, without thinking, usually. I'm very impulsive, I do a lot of stupid things, all the time. Although it's definitely been dangerous, sometimes being impulsive feels good. A lot of people say to me, 'My life's so boring.'

And I go, 'Yeah, it fucking is.' or 'What a fucking shame!'

A lot of my friends say to me, 'Oh god, I wished I could have done that.'

I say, 'Do it, darling, do it!' because, as far as I'm concerned, that's all there is to it.

I just think I'm very lucky I've had a great life, and I've had so much fun in it. My life is how it is, because I'm impulsive and I do things. People ask if I regret them, and I say, no. I just carry on with my life, with the next thing. I don't have any regrets because life is for living and, believe you me, I've bloody well lived.

I've always been impulsive, as far back as I can remember, so it must be part of the way I am. I don't have impulsive friends and I would never try to persuade anyone to be impulsive if it wasn't for them but, on the other hand, if someone is impulsive, then they should go for it – it's so liberating.

Friendships

Some of my friends want to be like me – I can tell by the things they say, asking me what I would do in their situation, or by telling me I'm so lucky to have done what I've done - but you know what? Nobody can be like me, and I don't mean that, arrogantly, I mean it kindly. I am me.

Don't try to copy someone else, be your own person. You never know, you might be better than me – but I bloody well doubt it!

No, seriously, I think everyone should find out who they are, and try to be that person the best way they can.

I'm lucky because I've always been very headstrong, confident, and outgoing. I talk to anyone, and I've just become more like that over the years. Some people take time to work out who they are, what they want to be, but the worst thing is to try and copy someone else – oh, no.

Anything I would Change About Myself?

This will probably sound arrogant, but I wouldn't change anything, because I'm happy who I am. I don't need to change anything. If you don't like me, I don't care. I am me, and you are you. I'm not perfect, but I'm a good laugh, I'm kind and generous, and with the world so full of bastards, that's not too bad, I reckon.

Relaxation

For me, the relaxation comes on my holidays and I really enjoy those. I usually have three to four holidays a year, a week to ten days each. I don't tend to like two-week holidays because I get a bit bored, just sitting around doing nothing.

Although I'm a workaholic when I'm on holiday, I try to switch off by reading, swimming, and enjoying myself, but it's quite difficult to turn the phone off. That, for me, is the most difficult thing in the world. I try not to check my work emails while on holiday. I always mean to have a total break, but soon my finger hovers over the email button on my phone. I think I don't want to, but I do, and then I'm reading and replying and deleting and God knows what with my work emails, while I'm sat by the pool with a book and a cocktail. It's madness, but that's me.

Grudges

I don't believe in holding grudges against people, it's a waste of energy and time, why bother? A friend once said the best revenge is to live well, and that's what I try and do. Let it bloody well go! Don't focus on the past and what went wrong. Move forward, think of the next exciting thing you can do in your life and go and bleedin' well do it!

Next?

I think next is one of the best words in the English language – it has so much possibility, so many options, so much optimism and hope. Next for me, who knows, who can say what I'll do next? But I'm sure I'll carry on working as I am now, both the cosmetic injectables, and the nursing, because I enjoy it and I'm good at it. I don't think I'll ever stop working, because I'm a workaholic – I'll still be working when they nail down the coffin and sling me into the ground!

My Next Husband

According to a clairvoyant, my next husband was coming June, July, or August 2016. I hope he's fucking handsome and has loads of money, because I am looking forward to someone who can look after me, sweep me off my feet and be worthy of being Husband Number Four.

Though as you can see, he's not yet arrived, so I'm still waiting for the next man in my life.

Pets

I've got two guard cats. They drive me round the fricking twist, but they are useful. One of them scratches to go out so I let him out, then he scratches to come in, so I let him in. All night, they're scratching and coming in and out, it's like some sort of a cat nightclub. They treat the house like a hotel – it's like having teenage children in the house again. I don't get any fricking sleep!

CHAPTER TWENTY THREE

Why me?

I think I exude a certain amount of sexuality and animal magnetism. I can pull someone when I want to. And I can talk and listen to anybody.

When I'm out on my own or even with friends, anybody will talk to me – I think I've got one of those faces that says, come talk to me, I'll listen.

One day, I was on a train going to down to London and a man in his sixties, bald head, dressed casually in a tracksuit, sat next to me at one stop and started talking. I always think it's more interesting to talk to people than sit in silence and read a bloody book, so I was listening to him. He didn't look posh or sexy but he was polite enough and didn't have bad body odour – so many people have such poor personal hygiene.

Anyway, he told me his name, then he said, 'I'm going to London to meet some friends today.'

'I'm going for a conference.' I asked the lady with the trolley for a cuppa tea and asked if the man wanted anything, on me – he seemed kind, and it's just like buying someone in a pub a drink, I do it all the time. He wanted a coffee and a Kit Kat so I bought it for him.

'Thanks,' he said, taking them from the lady. 'I haven't seen these friends in years.'.

'Why's that?' I thought he was going to say he'd lost touch, or they'd fallen out, something like that.

'I've been in prison for thirty five years for killing a member of my family.'

I thought, shit, how am I meant to get out of this one? Play it cool, cool as a cucumber. So I carried on listening and nodding as he talked and I drank my coffee.

'Oh, Mary, they've let me out today.' He broke the Kit Kat and offered me a finger.

I waved it away. 'That's for you, you enjoy it.' But inside I'm going, oh fucking hell, here we go again.

He told me about how he'd been driven to do it, how he didn't have any choice but to kill his brother. 'He was Mum's favourite, see, so I had to show her.'

'What did you show her?' I was a bit more relaxed by now, because he hadn't pulled a knife on me or anything, so I thought I'd go with it and humour him.

'I was better than him.'

There was no answer to that, so I just stared out the window at the fields whizzing past, wishing we were nearer to London.

He told me about his time in prison, how he was high security and had been gradually moved to lower and lower security. 'For good behaviour. At the end, it was like a holiday camp. Except I couldn't leave, but almost the same.' He laughed.

I thought well, he can't be too bad. And still no sign of a knife or a gun.

When we arrived in London, he asked me how to get to Trafalgar Square because that was where he was meeting his friends.

'I don't know London well, I usually get taxis, but I think there's a tube station. You're best off asking someone at the station.' I squeezed past him, said goodbye and left him talking to the train guard about Trafalgar Square station.

Nice enough bloke but, out of the whole train, why did he have to sit next to me?

My last lodger had just left, so I put an advert on this website advertising a room for rent, to get another one. I was inundated with people, but one guy had phoned me to talk about it, and then he went onto WhatsApp and started sending me messages and other things.

I deleted everything, because he didn't want to rent the room, but he kept sending me messages, which was annoying because I really didn't want to hear from him again.

A couple of days later, I went to work and I was showing the girls the pictures of my daughter's dog on my phone. 'This is Charlie, this is Charlie, oh dear, that's not Charlie!' It was a picture of a penis. That freaked me out, because I didn't know how it had got there, especially after I'd deleted all his messages to me. I hadn't even noticed he'd sent me any pictures. I didn't even know who he was, and he'd sent me quite a few pictures of his penis! I'm quite broad minded, and I've certainly seen a cock or two in my time, but not from a complete stranger I'd never met. The fact that I hadn't asked to see his cock, too, is what upset me. It felt like he was flashing me, only into my phone.

I found out where he worked and managed to get his boss's name and number. I gave the police all the information.

But the biggest clue was that he had his name tattooed on the top of his leg. I left it a while, but it had been playing on my mind, so eventually I ended up at the cop shop to report it. When I turned up, the police officer came out and said, 'Sorry to have kept you waiting, my name's PC Allcock.'

'Are you taking the piss?'

'What do you mean?'

'I've come in here with a load of willies on my phone, and they send me an Allcock.'

'Madam, that is my name, and it is not related to the obscene pictures you are alleging to have on your phone.'

Anyway, this PC Allcock took a statement and we went through the whole scenario from start to finish, then I printed off all these pictures for evidence.

I'd been there for an hour or so with the PC by this point. 'Look, I can't call you Allcock, I'm gonna call you Rob. You're gonna have to take me home, you know. Go and tell the sergeant you're taking me home.'

We're in the car and I'm going, 'Put your foot down!'

'What?' He looked at me.

'We're in a bloody police car, nobody's gonna stop us, put your foot down!'

He was pootling along at twenty miles an hour — I wanted him to get a move on and make the most of being in a cop car.

When we eventually arrived at my house, about a day later it seemed, he let me out.

'Can you see why the pictures freaked me out? I'm pretty remote here, out of the way. I thought he was in the bushes spying on me or something.'

'I've made a note of it, Madam,' he said, then drove off.

Weeks later, I had a call from the police station. What happened is, they wanted this community resolution which actually meant Jack shit, so they phoned me up and said, 'Can you come into the station now?'

'Why?' Because I'd heard nothing from then since giving my statement.

'He's turned it round, saying that you're the perpetrator and he's the victim.'

'How's he managed that?' My hand was shaking as it rested on the kitchen work surface.

'I'm not able to tell you that over the phone. If you could come down to the station now, madam, I can explain.'

'Right, I'm bringing somebody with me tomorrow.' I slammed the phone down and rang my doctor friend, asked him to come with me. He's good with the police because he's posh and has been involved with them professionally, so he knows the tricks they try to pull.

So I took my friend with me and I said, 'Right, you can speak for me. This is what I want.'

My doctor friend explained for me I didn't want any of this community resolution bollocks, and I was the victim because they weren't pictures of my penis on my phone. And I got a written apology, and a promise he would never do it again.

After all that, I managed to get a new lodger called Nigel. After dickpic-gate I thought I'd wind up the neighbours about my new lodger. I was still a bit worried about my safety, even though the police were investigating it, and said I had no reason to be, but I still felt a bit vulnerable.

I went round to my neighbours. I said, 'I've got something to tell you.'

'What? Is everything all right?'

'I've had to take some drastic action after the obscene pictures.'

'What do you mean?' They knew about the obscene pictures because I'd gone round and told them at the time. I was actually quite upset when it was happening. Now I can laugh about it.

'I've hired a bodyguard,' I said.

And they looked at me, mouths open.

I was trying not to laugh – like I'd hire a bodyguard!

'Oh. If that's what you think best.'

'I need one.' I turned to walk back home.

'What's his name?'

'Bodyguard.' I couldn't think of anything else and expected them to realise I was pulling their legs.

'Interesting name.'

'I've got him from an agency, they've not told me his name yet. It's Bodyguards Inc.' I could hardly keep a straight face at this point.

'What car does he drive?'

'The bodyguard's car. Like the car in the film with Whitney Houston.'

'Take care.' They waved me home.

Anyway, when Nigel the lodger, turned up later, I said to him, 'You're the bodyguard.'

'You what?' he asked.

I explained what I'd told the neighbours, and asked if he'd play along with it.

He just shrugged. He had this big blacked-out window Audi which was exactly the sort of car I meant when I told the neighbours.

One evening, I walked into the lounge and there was a little black thing flying around. I had the patio doors open because it was a warm summer evening. I watched this thing as it swooped from one side of the room to the other. 'What's that?'

My son, Joseph, hadn't noticed it, even though he'd been sitting in the lounge all evening. 'What?'

'That!' I pointed to the black thing flying around. It had a small wing span, probably about nine inches.

'It's a bat,' he said, turning back to the TV.

'Don't just sit there, bloody well get rid of it! I don't want it making a nest here.' I wasn't sure if bats made nests or how they lived really, all I knew was I didn't want the bloody thing in my lounge.

Joseph stood on the sofa to reach it, but it just flew away.

I stood at one end of the lounge and Joseph stood at the other, and we walked together holding saucepans and buckets and flapping them. It just flew up to the ceiling and then hung from the bricks on the chimney breast, upside down. They do hang upside down, like in all the cartoons – so I did know something about bats.

'Must have flown down the chimney!' I said.

It was a new house, so there were no beams or thatched roof or cobwebs in nooks and crannies for it to be attracted to. Who knows why it wanted to join us in our lounge?

In the end, Joseph caught it in his fishing net and set it free into the garden. Never mind Free Willy, it was Free Batty in our house that night.

A few summers ago, at the peak of Fifty Shades of Grey when everyone was reading it, I went to my local Ann Summers shop.

It was standing room only, a long queue of people at the till. The rest of the shop was heaving with people looking at the handcuffs, little leather riding crops to discipline people with, and a pile of porn DVDs too.

I was at the front of the queue and the cashier opened the till, which was so stuffed with notes she could hardly close the drawer.

'You've had a good day.' I pointed at the cash.

'It's that book. We should be paying the author royalties too!'

That book was everywhere. Earlier that year, when I was on holiday with my daughter, Kate, in Egypt, we saw a massive body builder, covered in tattoos, reading it by the pool.

I said to Kate, 'Get a photograph, he's obviously in touch with his feminine side.'

Back in the Ann Summers shop, I said to the cashier that I'd read all three of the books.

I put my four pots of Pleasure Gel on the desk. I was so pleased with this gel I wanted to buy my three friends some, too. It's minty, tingly and only costs a tenner a pot.

The cashier picked up one pot then looked at me. 'It's not edible any more, madam.'

'Fuck, that's a blow because I'm using it as part of a calorie controlled diet!'

The cashier didn't know what to say, so she just scanned the four pots then took my money.

I don't know why suddenly that summer everyone was reading Fifty Shades of Grey. But I must admit, it was easy reading and it was quite a good story and I enjoyed everybody talking about it. It was nice to be able to talk to strangers about something you both had in common. Obviously it wasn't real, it was all complete fantasy. I'm sure you don't get people like the man and woman. Not in real life anyway!

I haven't seen anybody from school for a while. I've been getting on with my life. I think if you're meant to stay in touch with people from the past, you will stay in touch with them. Out of the blue, an old school friend had her birthday and her husband was organising the party. He called me. 'Will you come to Sophie's birthday?'

So I went to the birthday party and I didn't want to drink anything but, as usual, I ended up having a few drinks. It was full of people I couldn't remember and didn't want to talk to, so I thought a few vodkas would grease the old wheels a bit. It certainly felt more fun after I'd had a couple of drinks.

I explained I'd had a few and didn't want to risk losing my licence driving home, and could they order me a taxi.

'Oh, you're going to stay the night,' Sophie said. 'You'll never get a taxi at this time. Besides, it'll cost you a fortune. Waste of money.'

'OK.'

'Oh, so and so's in that room, so and so's in that room. Oh well, you can stay with us.'

'In your bed?' It seemed a bit odd.

'Oh, nothing sexual, it's just needs must, like camping when we were kids.'

And I didn't think anything more of it – she was an old school friend, remember, and her husband had been friendly to me earlier during the night, making sure I had enough to drink and introducing me to people I couldn't remember the names of.

And the next minute I was in bed with Sophie and her husband. Sophie was in the middle, I was on one side, and her husband was on the other.

I was trying to get to sleep, but the next minute I felt a big hand crawling over my breasts, then my stomach. His hand went down towards my vagina.

I grabbed the hand, screaming, 'Fuck off!' Then the lights came on.

Sophie sat up in bed, and stared at her husband.

I pulled the covers up around myself. 'What's he doing that for?'

'What?' she asked.

'Trying to grope me. In the dark!'

'I didn't,' he said.

'Maybe I brushed you,' Sophie said.

'You must think I was born bleedin' yesterday. It was a hand. I felt a hand on my tits and then my fanny. A big hairy hand.'

'Wasn't me,' he said, quickly hiding his hands underneath the duvet.

'It's been a long night,' she said. 'Let's get off to sleep.' She switched the light off.

I lay there, stiff as a board, worried the hand would make a reappearance. It didn't, or at least not while I was awake anyway.

I left the next morning and neither of them mentioned it, and so I didn't either. It was almost like an out of body experience because I was laying there thinking – this can't be happening to me.

After the great time I'd had from internet dating, I thought I'd help my friends by taking them speed dating. So I drove them to this town hall, paid for them to get in, bought them drinks. I'd read about it in a magazine and suggested it to my friends. 'It's just what you need. Get you out of the dating doldrums. Come along, meet someone, it'll be a laugh,' I said.

Little did I know.

It was a fucking awful evening. You sit opposite a man and chat to him for two minutes, then all the men stand up and move round one seat and you've got a new man to talk to – for another two minutes. I mean, what can you get to know about someone in that time?

They gave us a little marks sheet so you could rate the men for different categories – humour, looks, personality, things like that. I felt like I was back at bloody school, never mind on a night out with my friends.

I sat there, sober as a judge, with this parade of men appearing before me for two minutes at a time, answering the same bloody two or three questions every time. I was thinking how kind I'd been to my friends and how fucking bored I was. I checked the time and we'd only been there for half an hour, and still had another hour and a half to go. I waved at one of my friends, and gestured that I was going out for a cigarette. I stood.

The man sat opposite me said, 'Who am I meant to talk to in this two minutes?'

'Talk to who you like, love, because I'm not interested. I'm having a fag.' I left the hall and stood outside, smoking a cigarette, wondering where I'd gone wrong and remembering what my mother always used to tell me – no good deed goes unpunished.

Bloody right too.

As I walked back inside, a big black man bumped into me. I could tell he was deaf and dumb because he was signing to someone on his phone. Takes all sorts, I thought. As he got closer I thought, I recognise your face. Turned out he was one of my patients, when I worked at the walk in centre.

I went back to my seat, rolled my eyes at the new bloke sat there, and told him to get on with it because I didn't have all bloody evening.

On the way home in the car, my friends were very quiet so I asked them how they'd got on. 'Meet anyone nice you're gonna see again?'

'Mary, how much can you get to know about someone in two minutes?'

The other friend chipped in with, 'Just as I was getting to know them, they'd off and leave and I'd be back to square one again with the next one.'

I banged the steering wheel. 'Precisely!'

'Thank God I was drinking. Christ knows what sort of a night you had.'

'You can thank me later,' I said, and we drove back and never spoke about it again.

I was booked on a flight to Belfast for a weekend, visiting a man I'd met online. I arrived at the check in desk, and handed over my passport and email confirmation.

The woman tapped the computer, stared at the screen then said, 'I'm afraid madam, we can't check you in.'

'Why not? I've bought a flight and I want to go on it.' I pulled myself up to the desk and eyed up the name of the woman from her badge.

'You have, madam, but your ticket is for this date next month.'

I checked my email and she was bloody well right. I sagged a bit.

'It will cost £300 to change the ticket.'

I'd only paid about fifty quid for the ticket so I thought, sod that, and booked a new one. 'I'll probably come back a month later too – Belfast is a fun city so why not visit it again.'

She eyed me up then pointed to the departure gate.

I walked along the aisle and took my seat.

After a while, a couple of business men stood next to my seat. 'I think you're sat in our seat.'

I knew I wasn't, so I said, 'I'm not, you know. You must have it wrong.' I folded my arms and stared straight ahead, trying to pretend they weren't there.

They kept showing me their tickets so, after a while, I checked mine and finally said, 'Yes, you're right, thank you very much!' And I left them to it, feeling mortified with embarrassment.

When I found my actual right seat, an Irish man called Jo sat next to me. He had no teeth.

'Why haven't you got any teeth, are you scared of the dentist?'

'I am, and I think you've been sent by God to make me go to the dentist.'

'And you've been sent to get me through this bleedin' flight.'

When we landed, we went for a drink and had some Irish stew at the pub. He told me his life story. He'd led a hard life so I wasn't surprised he didn't have perfect teeth. When I told him about Dr Mohammed who ripped me off and made me go bankrupt, it turned out Jo knew him – how's that for coincidence?

After a few days away, a taxi dropped me off at Belfast airport. I walked into the building and I couldn't see my flight. I was looking through the signs and checking the email with the details, but still couldn't see my flight.

'Where's my flight?' I asked the woman at the help desk.

She checked my email. 'You've missed your flight, it's at the other airport.'

Who knew Belfast had two airports? Not me! I snatched the email back. 'I bleedin' well have not.' Ran out the airport, said to the taxi drivers, 'Right, who's Sterling Moss?'

One of them put his hand up so I jumped into his taxi.

He rushed me to the other Belfast airport, and told me his life story in twenty minutes on the way.

I ran up to the desk for my flight, and handed my passport and email over.

'You're cutting it fine,' the woman said, checking the time. 'Ten minutes until the gate closes.'

'Thank you!' I ran all the way to the gate just as they were closing, caught my breath, and said to the air steward as I boarded the plane, 'You're not gonna believe what happened to me.' I could hardly catch my breath.

'Went to the wrong airport, did you?'

'How'd you know?'

'Happens all the time.' She showed me to my seat.

Sitting in the seat next to mine was a handsome hunk of a body builder with really nice teeth.

I sat next to him and smiled. 'Nice body, you're better than the man I sat next to on the way out, he didn't have any teeth.'

'Thanks, I do weight lifting.'

As the flight went on, he started talking about his gym routine, how often he went, which weights he lifted, and one thing and another. 'Do you want to see it?' He flexed his biceps at me.

'What?'

'My chest?' He winked at me.

'Go on then. No point all your hard work being covered up.'

He took his top off and showed me his chest. It was bulging with muscles and covered in tattoos. He looked like a He-Man cartoon, with a nice face and white teeth.

'Anabolic steroids?' I said.

'I don't touch that shit. This is all my own hard work.'

'Fair enough. Have you got any designer underpants on?' We were a bit pissed by this point, and I was enjoying flirting with him so I thought I'd push my luck some more.

He thought about it for a bit. "I have, as it happens. I won them in a body building competition.'

'Don't tell me, show me. And I want a pair of them as a souvenir.'

He left for the toilet and after a while returned, handing me a tissue.

'What the hell's this?'

'I've only brought two pairs of underpants, so I can't give you one.' He was travelling to Birmingham to meet a girlfriend who was then going to Spain with him.

'Look, if you're in trouble in Birmingham, give me a ring and I'll sort things out for you.'

He kissed me on the lips and said, 'I'll definitely see you again and keep in touch.'

We stayed in touch for about a year, texting and talking on the phone.

Recently Kate saw a picture of him on my phone and asked for his number. 'That body's like a Greek statue or something. It's so sculpted.'

'He's too old for you.'

'How old is he?' she asked.

'Thirty three and I want him for myself!'

'Fair enough.'

This is what happens to me on flights when I'm on my own. On another flight, I sat next to a seventy year old man flying to Turkey. There was no booze because it was Ramadan. I'd started talking to this man and we were having a right laugh, getting to know each other, asking why was he flying to Turkey, and I told him about my Turkish husband who I was visiting.

I sweet-talked the air steward. 'I'm flying with my very good friend and we haven't seen each other for many years. He hasn't long to live, he's been told. I know it's Ramadan, but would you let us have a few of those tiny little bottles of vodka so we can have a drink and a catch up together?'

'We don't normally allow it, madam, because it's Ramadam,' she replied.

'I understand, it's just this trip is on his bucket list and he's going to actually kick the bucket quite soon. We'll be quiet, I promise.'

I jingled the cups of ice and pulled a few bottles of vodka out of my handbag.

Well, by a few bottles in, I made him laugh so much his fake teeth flew out and landed on the floor. 'I'm so sorry, I didn't mean to!' He was looking on the floor trying to find them.

'It's nothing to me, darling, I'm a nurse, I'm fine.' I popped his teeth straight back in and we carried on laughing.

CHAPTER TWENTY FOUR

Mary's words of wisdom – Part Three

Regrets

My life has been so funny and so interesting that I wouldn't want to do anything again or do anything differently. I think everything I've done, it's all been done for a reason. My nursing led to the cosmetics work, which meant I could put both my kids through private school, which was the best thing I could've done, because they've done so well, they're so privileged. It was definitely money well spent. I don't regret any of my husbands or relationships, because they've all given me something, taught me something, which has made me move onto the next thing. As for Husband Number Two, although not a very nice marriage, if it weren't for him, I wouldn't have Joseph and Kate, so even him, I don't regret. I don't do regrets really. What's the point? You can't go back and change something, so you might as well learn from the shit life's put you through, and move on.

My Heroines

Margaret Thatcher, without doubt, is my heroine. What an amazing lady, but sadly not with us any longer. I saw the film with Meryl Streep, but it was only OK – it didn't really do her justice, I thought.

She was an amazing woman, she did so much for the UK when we were fucked as a country in the seventies. We had strikes, people not burying dead bodies, not collecting rubbish, not building bloody cars – it was a fucking mess. She came along and she sorted it all out. We've not had a prime minister since who's changed Britain and where it is in the world as much as she did. And it bloody well needed changing!

She won three general elections by a massive majority, I think. The Falklands War – she did exactly what needed doing, to teach the Argentinians we meant business. The Miners' Strike – she held onto her beliefs it was the right thing for the country, and saw it through to the end.

I think she was a bit like me, when she liked someone, she lays on the praise, can't say enough about how great the person is, but when she didn't think much of someone, she could be cutting with her criticism.

I like someone who doesn't mince their words. There's too much mollycoddling around, not saying what needs to be said. If you get it out in the open, everyone knows what you're on about.

Thatcher never held back from saying what she thought. That's a great quality, I think. I know there are a lot of people who didn't like her.

When she died, somebody on my Facebook was saying the most hurtful things, you know, ding dong the witch is dead, and good riddance to bad rubbish, that sort of thing. I just deleted her from my Facebook because it was unnecessary, it was disrespectful. Someone's mum had just died and that deserved respect. I wasn't having that sort of crap on my Facebook, especially not about Margaret Thatcher.

She was like a world class battleship at full steam ahead, and that's something I admired in her, and which I try to do myself; when I put my mind to something I will make it happen, and I'm not easy to stop – like when I decided to do the cosmetics work, or put my children through private school. Thatcher wasn't easily stopped either, once she'd put her mind to something. Marvellous woman.

Margaret Thatcher was absolutely dynamic and brilliant at what she did. Growing up, I absolutely aspired to be like her. They called her the iron lady, so bloody focussed, a brilliant woman.

I also like Katie Price – I admire her, she looks absolutely stunning, especially considering she's had five fricking kids and she looks brilliant on it. Like Margaret Thatcher, Katie Price is a very strong dynamic person and I like that in a woman. Katie Price is a very clever business woman – her clothing businesses, her celebrity appearances, her books, her reality TV shows – it's all cleverly organised to make the most of herself and the people who love her, and to make money for her and her family. Brilliant woman.

I look up to these women because being driven, focused, and doing your best are important values for me, and these two women have those in buckets and buckets.

Being Determined

When I told my parents I wanted to train to be a nurse, although it was nothing like what they'd experienced, or anyone in their family had done before, they knew how determined I was. The thing is, if I put my mind to something, I will do it. Years ago, I had to do an IQ test for a job application and I remember testing my own IQ and I'm actually fucking Einstein! No, seriously, because I went through this book full of IQ tests and I kept doing it and doing it, and in the end my IQ was amazing! You can get your IQ pretty bloody high if you keep practising and practising! That's what I'm like – if I get an idea into my head about wanting to do something, I will work full steam ahead until I get it done; it's just who I am. I can't do anything any other way.

Marmite Mary

I'm a bit like Marmite, you either love me or you hate me. But you know, I've got to the stage in my life where I actually don't really care. I am what I am, darling! I'm loud, I'm opinionated, I'm a very sexual person, I'll always tell it how it is, and if you don't like that, then you'll probably hate me.

Over the years, I've actually changed. I used to worry about what people thought of me, wondering did I need to change to fit with what people wanted me to be like? But nowadays, I know that I'm a good person and would help anybody. I think that's my nursing – it's in me to help people. I've looked after all sorts of people while nursing, and I love to help people. I'm not going to pretend to be some little mousy person, someone I'm not. I am me, and I'm happy with that.

If you don't like me, then that's your tough luck.

Romance

I'm naturally optimistic about love and romance. A bit like Marilyn Monroe was, I suppose – she was married three times like me, too. Only I'm a natural true blonde, unlike Marilyn. I don't have any grey, I'm very lucky.

Even now, with men, I'm a bit of a romantic. I always believe he is The One. Even when I was flying all over the place doing the internet dating, although it was exciting to meet all these new men, at the back of my mind, along with the possibility of sex – and I do love sex, I'm a very physical person – the most important thing was the possibility of him being The One.

I know there will be Husband Number Four at some stage. I need to find somebody who's going to look after me, instead of me looking after him. That's what I want in a man. It's hard though, because I am so strong willed, such a forceful personality. I can't just go along with what a man wants, I have to do what I want. I have to say what I think, and not all men like that. Strong and flexible, that's what I want from a man like, I don't know, collagen injections – strong to plump me up, to make me look fabulous, to give my face some support, but flexible so he eventually dissolves! No, so he can fit around me and what I want, and me as a person. I don't know, it sounds too much to ask doesn't it? But I'm sure I will find it!

See, I'm always the optimist when it comes to love and romance.

Having Regrets

I don't really have any regrets and I don't think I'd actually change anything I've done in my past. Things always happen for a reason. No regrets, I get on with it and look forward to the next adventure.

You can't dwell on mistakes you've made, things that have gone wrong in your life. If you dwell on something it'll eat you away, let it go, move on, just forget it. I think this attitude has allowed me to move on with all the things that have happened in my life.

CHAPTER TWENTY FIVE

What I've learned from bankruptcy and divorce

I don't do regrets. I believe everything I've been through has led me to be the person I am now, and I wouldn't change anything about who I am. However, I have definitely learned things from the two most traumatic experiences of my life: bankruptcy and divorces. I'm a changed person from who I was before I went through these things. That's why I wouldn't regret going through either of them. I hope that makes sense. It does to me anyway!

The bankruptcy has affected my life for six years. From the moment of discharge in 2009, I had to wait until November 2015 before I could get rid of that black mark on my record. Now, after all that time, I'm credit worthy again.

Bankruptcy isn't an easy option. I hope I've showed this in the earlier chapter when I described what it felt like at the time. It's not just a form to fill in and magically all the debts go away. No fear! It's stressful to go through from start to finish. It affects you for years afterwards and it's not something anyone should go through without thinking about it very carefully first.

Going bankrupt means you've got to be so careful with money. You can't borrow any money. No credit cards, no loans, nothing. It taught me to live within my means for once. It taught me to only buy things when I had the money for them. It made me realise the actual value of money itself. Instead of a number on a form when I was applying for a loan – which felt unreal – since then I've had to work out my budget each month and stick to it. It's taught me to manage my own business in a better financial way than I did when I worked with the doctor. I now take responsibility for my own money and try to do everything to avoid getting into debt.

I kept my current mortgage, even though I had a lot of problems when I nearly walked away from it all. It's still interest only and I've never reversed it to repayment, because I'm hoping I won't need to. I'm hoping my next husband will be rich enough and kind enough to take care of the mortgage and me.

Is that good financial planning? I'm not sure, but it's about as much planning as I'm going to do anyway. I know I will never get into such terrible debt again. Now that I can borrow money again, I actually don't want to. I can't think of anything worse than having loans around my neck like I had before.

If I could talk to myself now? If I knew what I know now about bankruptcy, I would have actually tried to prevent it. I know this goes against my theory of everything that doesn't kill you, makes you stronger, but honestly, the bankruptcy was so terrible I never want to go through it again.

I actually didn't know how much debt I was in. It really did accumulate very quickly. Only on the final day did I think, how the hell am I going to be able to pay this money back?

I'm very much more careful now. I'm still a bit too generous for my own good. I've always been generous and I still am. I wouldn't get a car loan. I have credit cards but I have no loans and only the mortgage. The car I have now, I bought with cash a year ago. But hopefully the next car won't cost me a penny, if Husband Number Four turns up!

I actually find the concept of debt very stressful. I like to know what I'm paying. I hate being ripped off. I was far too blasé with money when I started doing Botox, because it was relatively new treatment, and I used to walk around with thousands of pounds in my handbag.

Nowadays, I've got a book keeper and other people in place to keep me in the black financially.

I've definitely lived a more interesting life than my parents, with my jobs and business, but I'm sure they'd be horrified if they knew some of the things I got up to and have confessed in this book! But that wouldn't stop me from doing them again! In case you haven't realised, I live my life pretty much without fear. If I want to do something, I just do it. I don't spent hours and hours, or days and weeks, wondering if I'm going to do something. I just get on and bleedin' well do it.

A friend once told me that some people spend their whole lives putting things off. Telling themselves they'll do stuff when they're retired, when they have a new job, when they have enough money. Not me. I just grab life by the cock and balls and do it now. I'm like that famous sports brand, I just get on and do it.

The three divorces have taught me a whole load of things. That's why I wouldn't do any of them any differently. I've learned so much. I'm a much wiser woman for having gone through the divorces.

Were they stressful at the time? Yes.

Do I regret getting married in the first place? Not at all.

Most women I talk to who have had husbands and got a divorce, they seem to get a payout. I've never had that. People have always taken me to the cleaners during a divorce. Am I bitter about that? No.

Sometimes when I hear about someone who's done very well financially out of a divorce but I haven't, I admit that I do get pissed off.

I will definitely get married again. I'm in awe of people, like my mum and dad, who stuck it out for fifty years married. The endurance in that is incredible. Unbelievable, considering the longest I've managed to be married is twelve years!

I'm not cynical about marriage or men after the divorces. I'm very open minded. I'm in a good place at the moment. I'm having a lot of interest from people. I'm happy, considering the traumas I've been through.

In all honesty, I'm actually addicted to marriage. I love a bit of cake! I'm all for marriage, as an institution, as a concept. I love it.

I don't like the word partner. I just hate it. I'd much rather say, 'I've got a husband.'

Partner makes me think of a firm of solicitors, or working in a company together, not a relationship.

Three marriages and three divorces have taught me that I definitely like men. Maybe a bit too much.

I think women are possibly the stronger sex in a lot of ways.

Mentally stronger. But it hasn't put me off. The next husband, hopefully, won't be as young as the last one, and he'll hopefully be more respectful and treat me how I deserve to be treated. I don't want to be a man's punch bag. I've been that twice and that's enough for anyone.

Now that I look back at them all, I realise that each marriage ended for different reasons. The first one, he was like a brother to me really. He was a kind man but not the passionate man I wanted to stay with. I never wanted children with him. I think unconsciously I must have known I wasn't going to stay with him. And I'll be honest, I was never faithful to him, because he was so fucking boring. So in the end he divorced me for adultery. Sad, but there it is. I couldn't have stuck with him bored shitless for the rest of my life.

The second husband, he turned out to be a vile piece of shit. I definitely loved him at the start, but he was a bastard. He definitely had passion, a bit too much of it, if I'm honest. Anger. Lots of it. Violence and anger aren't passion, I now know. But after the physical and mental abuse, I just had enough, so I fell out of love with him. I now have two wonderful kids from that relationship who are my life. He's with someone else now. What a fucking shame for her, I say. Am I bothered that he's not with me? No. I'm relieved someone else has to deal with his anger and violence. I got what I needed out of him, some of his sperm, otherwise I wouldn't have my children. Even now I dislike him immensely. That may seem strange because I'm not with him anymore, but I think it's because the way he treated me was so terrible, that I can remember it like it happened yesterday. They say you should forgive, but may not forget. Well, I can't forget because it was so painful – his physical and mental cruelty to me. But also because it was so strong and went on for so long. I don't think, in my heart of hearts, I'll ever really be able to forgive him. Maybe there are other battered ex-wives out there who've been able to forgive, but not me, I'm afraid. I don't speak to him and yet I still feel this strongly about him. Strange isn't it? Not very spiritual is it? Well, you come back to me when you've been admitted to hospital by someone punching you to the ground when you're pregnant with his child, and then tell me how spiritual and forgiving you feel. Sometimes I wonder what I saw in him in the first place. I think it was his drive, his go get 'em attitude to work, and he was undoubtedly a much more interesting and passionate man than my first husband.

Then the Turkish man. Now I think back on it, he was way too young for me. There was a twenty year age gap between us. That's never going to work, is it? And, if I'm honest, I bought him. And then I paid to get rid of him. I bought him into what I thought was my designer lifestyle. I'd built the house. I'd got the hot tub, I'd got the sauna. I just needed that perfect designer man on my arm. He was very easy on the eye. He was a designer husband – to look at. He was loving, passionate, sexy and exactly what I thought I needed in a man. I was actually a bit crazy marrying him, actually. But unfortunately he was also immature, a gambler, a liar and a bit of a misogynist too, if I'm honest. I'm not sure if that was part of the culture of where he came from. In Turkey, they treat women differently from how they're treated in the UK. He expected me to do as he said, to be subservient to him, to let him do what the bloody hell he wanted. It was his right to do what he wanted and I should work around it. On paper, the odds of us being happy ever after with the age difference and the different attitudes to women, it just wasn't going to happen.

Three marriages, three divorces and my experiences with hundreds of other men, have taught me a lot about love. I can fall in love quite easily. I very much like the company of men. I've had a lot of men, sexually. I'm a trollop. There's no two ways about it, and I'm not ashamed of it. A man sleeps with lots of women, then he's a hero; a woman does it, and she's a slag.

And that's equality, is it?

I believe I am a man in a woman's body. I can do what a man does. I can have the sex and just walk away, without getting hung up on the emotions. Well, sometimes I've had trouble actually walking away afterwards, but that's another story! I separate sex and love very easily.

Despite this, I'm still a very female woman in the traditional way – I like to dress up, take care of my appearance, I like a gossip and a chat with friends, I enjoy a girly film and book, and shopping for shoes. All those stereotypical female things – I love them all.

But in some ways, I've got a lot of male inside me. And I don't just mean when I'm having sex!

All of this has taught me that I want some more wedding cake! I definitely want to do it again – the whole marriage, wedding, husband thing. I'm hoping it's going to be fourth time lucky!

I've tried it three times and haven't yet succeeded, but that's not going to stop me trying. Even after three husbands, I am a firm believer in marriage because it's wonderful – wonderful to be legally with someone, wonderful to have a husband, and not just a boyfriend or a partner – always sounds a bit like a business partner. Wonderful to have the opportunity to tell everyone how much you love your husband; wonderful to formalise your love for someone, when so much nowadays is so informal. Wonderful.

I feel hopeful about marriage because I am generally an optimistic person, including marriage and love, and I'm always thinking this man is going to be the next perfect husband. For me, that's the best word in the world – next. Just like in the rest of my life, I don't regret any of my marriages, I've had fun and learnt things, and had children, all different experiences from each of my three marriages, but I wouldn't go back, no chance. An ex is an ex for a reason, and I'll leave it at that.

I think I've been in love with the idea of marriage more than the man I'm actually married to. I'm hoping the next man I find will love me for who I am, for the real whole, unapologetic me, and want to look after me.

I realise I am very much a control freak and I really need to step back a bit. I'm expecting there will be another man, and the next one will be forever. Somebody that can look after me, instead of me always being in control. I've always been in control. I want somebody to look after me for a bit.

I think my expectations of a man and marriage are realistic. I've seen plenty of friends happily married for years. So why not me, eh?

I believe a marriage should be a partnership, where you can work together, love each other and respect each other as equals.

I've never had that.

I'm a very strong woman and I think I intimidate some men. I'm not the easiest person to get on with, I'll admit that. I am opinionated. I'm loud. I'm forceful. I am a passionate woman. But I do have good qualities. I'm very kind. I'll always help people and I'll always stick up for the underdog.

One of my best qualities as a wife is definitely my humour. I love a good joke, especially when other people laugh. If they don't laugh, that pisses me off. I was in a pub in Wales and I was in the middle of telling a joke, and a man interrupted me.

'You're a farmer, I can tell, you smell of shit. Now fuck off!'

A woman with a sense of humour is difficult for a lot of men. I like to laugh. It's so therapeutic as well. Some men see it as a threat. Some insecure men. But I don't give a shit.

I'm also a very passionate woman. Not many men can keep up with me – in the bedroom and out of it!

So watch this space. Applications for Husband Number Four are being received now!

Even if I could go back to my nineteen year old self, when I married my first husband, I still wouldn't do anything differently. Not the marriages, the affairs, the divorces, not any of it. Whatever I've gone through, if it's not killed me (which nothing has yet!) then it's made me stronger. My children are my life, even though I hate their guts and they hate mine! JOKING! I really wanted them to go to a private school because I couldn't go to one myself. And that was what made me venture into Botox and aesthetics all those years ago. Without them, I wouldn't be the Botox Babe I am today. My daughter is basically a mini me, and that's why we clash so much!

My strength to continue through all the ups and downs of my life comes from my parents, even though sadly they're both dead. Mum was a very strong woman. She was the dominator in the relationship. Mum had the quick brain and Dad had the humour. I get my strength from them. I firmly believe they're somewhere looking out for me.

I'm hopeful that I'll find a man as passionate as I am, but I definitely won't be pursuing him so frantically through internet dating as I have before. Instead, I'm going to be letting Fate take its time. In the meantime, I'm very loved by my friends and family, and have plenty of men I can call on for sex, because I'm a very physical woman and I need that!

CHAPTER TWENTY SIX

Now, and why I'm still a Botox Babe

I'd been talking to a man I met online. He was calling me all the time, telling me he loved me. He kept saying he wanted to meet me and that he loves me. We'd been talking for ages on the phone, and he said, 'I'll meet you when I'm next in the UK and I want to buy you a car.'

I had my eyes on this brand new red Mercedes offroader and he said he'd buy it for me. Big thing, it was, high up off the road.

It was difficult to meet him because he was always here, there, and everywhere for business. He was a banker, or an investor, or something. Anyway, there I was, thinking – this is it, this is Husband Number Four and he's going to be brilliant!

Well, it turned out he was only a scammer, wasn't he? A professional scammer. I've got a solicitor I'm speaking to about getting my money back. This dream man, he's got me for money.

'I need you to send me some money for a business transaction I'm in the middle of. I will give it straight back, I promise. I love you, darling,' he said. It was regarding this, and regarding the other.

And do you know what? I only went and gave him the money! I hope I can get the deposit for this Merc back from the garage. I'll just explain I've changed my mind, and it wasn't much money anyway. But the man, he's taken me for quite a bit actually.

I'm dangerous. Don't let me have any money! If I've got money, I'm stupid. I can't believe I've done what I have. I thought I'd have learned after going bankrupt, but I suppose it's the love addict and optimist in me that's taken over this time! I've got this red light on my head – anyone wants to scam me, I'm an idiot and

I fall for it every fucking time.

It's because I'm hopeful and optimistic. I didn't see this coming. It's something else I've got to deal with. There's always another challenge I've got to deal with in my life. But, what doesn't kill me makes me stronger, that's what I always say!

I'm still very busy work wise. I'm working like I always do, which is every day. I'm a workaholic. Always have been, always will be. I'm working in the plastic surgery hospital in Birmingham two days a week, which is really nice. I'm still doing the NHS work eight and a half hours a week, plus my own aesthetics business which has gone absolutely ballistic at the moment.

In an average week, I probably do between ten and twenty hours of aesthetics. All of a sudden, it's gone really busy. My most popular procedure is, as always, Botox. Cheeks and Botox. In an average month I'm seeing twenty clients for aesthetics. Well, I need to get back the money that I keep giving away!

So that's why I'm still a Botox Babe, and why I'll carry on being one for the foreseeable future. I don't know if I'd have more surgery in the future. I've no plans for it at the moment. I may have my arms done at some stage. Because as a lady gets older, the upper arms can get a bit saggy. They call them the bye byes, because when you wave goodbye, they swing from side to side. I'm not that bad at the moment, but I don't want to look my age. Don't get me wrong, I don't think that I'm dysmorphic. I don't think I look in the mirror and think I look terrible. I mean my appearance doesn't bother me. I'm happy with how I look at the moment.

I think I've got this energy for life, living, laughing, and there's always something else to come, isn't there? I can feel it in myself, there's still plenty more adventures to come!

At the moment, my love life's been pretty quiet. I've been seeing somebody for a bit of fun, but nothing serious. Although I'm still looking for the next husband. Whether it will happen any time soon, I don't know. I think it will. I'm sure it will.

I don't like odd numbers so there's got to be a fourth. I thought I'd met the next husband – the rich businessman who was jetting all over the world — but he turned out to be a scammer.

I think the next man has got to be somebody in the medical profession. Somebody where we're on the same wavelength. Somebody who's going to stop me being such a twat! It's the second time I've fallen for a scam. I think I'm a bit stupid sometimes. I said, I need to dye my hair, because I am mentally blonde. On second thoughts, maybe I'm not stupid, I'm just too trusting. Not with business – I'm very astute now with that, since the money problems before. But with love I am too trusting. And all my clothes fall off all the time.

My life with friends and family is lovely, very fulfilling, varied, exciting, interesting. I have friends I've known for a long time, and who I know I can rely on. I want to count my blessings. I have got a lot of friends who I enjoy spending time with, doing all sorts of things. Some I go on holiday with, others are there for a quick trip to the hairdressers, or maybe a good old booze up on the town. The people who used to really piss me off, I just got rid of them. It's the only way I've found that works. I don't have time to be doing with people who piss me off.

My daughter and son haven't called me, so that's good. They obviously don't want any money, so they're fine! No, seriously, I'm very proud of them both and I'm so pleased I was able to give them a better education than I had. That, I firmly believe, is why they're both doing so well now.

I'm exactly where I expected to be at this stage in my life. I'm alive and that is a blessing. I'm lucky, even though I'm an idiot. Only the good die young, and clearly I've not been good, so I'll probably live to about a hundred and ten. I've done loads of things that have risked my life. Getting on a plane to meet random people in random countries.

My life is a work in progress, but isn't everyone's?

A husband would make my life complete now. My mission is to find a man who is not going to rip me off. But I don't think that's going to happen for a while now. I need to ring up that clairvoyant and give her a bollocking! She said, 'The man of your dreams is coming into your life in October.'

Oh, I thought, he's arrived, oh, even better, he's buying me a car! And then, oh no, he isn't.

I'm not going to put my life on hold in the meantime, while

I'm waiting for a man. And neither should anyone else. I've got lots of things to do. I won't go out of my way to look for a man. I think somebody will arrive. I don't think I'll go back to internet dating this week, but tomorrow's another day.

Life's for living, whether you're in a relationship or single. I don't think anyone should sit around waiting for a man, but don't let that stop you grabbing one if he passes! I will grab Husband Number Four when he comes along, but in the meantime, I'll carry on grabbing life by the balls every hour of every single day!

Lots of love,
Lady Mary, the Botox Babe
xxx

Printed in Great Britain
by Amazon